COMMON SENSE
INCOME STRATEGIES

COMMON SENSE

Simple Step-by-Step Ways

INCOME

to Maximize Your Retirement

STRATEGIES

Michael Eastham, CPA, PFS

PRESS

COMMON SENSE INCOME STRATEGIES

Published by
ADVISORS' ACADEMY PRESS
Pompano Beach, Florida

ISBN 978-0-9975441-4-5
Ebook ISBN 978-0-9975441-5-2

FIRST EDITION

Book Design by Neuwirth & Associates
Jacket Design by Tim Green

Manufactured in the United States of America

10 9 8 7 6 5 4 3 2 1

To my parents who set a wonderful
example for me to follow.

CONTENTS

· FOREWORD ·

David Scranton

Despite what some brokers and financial advisors might try to tell you, there is no single "secret" or "key" to successful saving and investing. Yet I know, just as Michael Eastham knows, from years of experience that there are certain ingredients or elements that can greatly improve your odds of success, and it just so happens that three of them are mentioned in the main title of Michael's book: common sense, income and strategy.

It's amazing to me how many smart people manage to neglect common sense when it comes to managing their money. (Well, maybe not so amazing when you consider the culture we live in, where aggressive marketing and slick salesmen can often distract consumers from their own good instincts, their "gut feeling," in other words.) Here is just one example of what I'm talking about: common sense *should* dictate that the closer one gets to retirement, the more important it is, to put protecting your existing wealth ahead of acquiring more wealth as a priority. Not that the second doesn't remain important, just no longer *more* important as the first!

The reason for this is fairly obvious: As you've been building your existing wealth over 30-to-40 years, you've been steadily losing another valuable commodity: *Time.* You no longer have "plenty" of it to recoup a major financial loss if you should suffer one within ten or fifteen years of retirement. Consequently, you might end up having to dramatically alter your retirement plans, abandon some of your retirement goals, or even put off retirement. (The common extreme example some advisors like to use is that you might end up "eating cat food." I don't think it actually comes to that very often, but you get the point!)

Thus, common sense *should* tell you that protecting your assets becomes increasingly important after age 50. Yet I know from experience that many people well into their 60s are still focused more on growth, than on protection. For whatever reason, be it Wall Street hype or a bad advisor, they are ignoring common sense and running an unnecessarily high risk of facing one of more of those unfortunate consequences I mentioned above.

How do "income" and "strategy" factor into it? Well, that question actually speaks to the genius of Michael's book. Because once you embrace common sense and make protection your top financial goal, you quickly realize that the key to achieving that goal lies in having an investment *strategy* specifically designed to generate dependable, sustainable retirement *income*. Voila! All three ingredients are interconnected—and there you have it.

Well, you really just have the beginning of it. Fortunately, you are also holding a book written by a man uniquely qualified to explain all the details. I'm talking about details that have actually changed lives, and allowed thousands of everyday investors, just like you, to avoid financial disaster and achieve their retirement goals with fearlessness and peace of mind.

To me, Michael Eastham is first and foremost a friend, but he also happens to be one of the most knowledgeable investment experts I know and one of the most engaging and effective communicators I have ever met. I'm thrilled that he's finally sharing his gifts with a broad, national audience through this book—particularly in light of the unprecedented levels of uncertainty and instability we're seeing in the global financial markets today. To put it simply, the need for investors over 50 to understand and focus on "Common Sense Income Strategies" has never been more important!

David J. Scranton, CLU, ChFC, CFP, CFA, MSFS
Host of *The Income Generation*
Author of *Return on Principle: Seven Core Values to Help Protect Your Money in Good Times and Bad*

COMMON SENSE
INCOME STRATEGIES

SECTION I
MAKING SENSE OF COMMON SENSE

· 1 ·

What Investors Want Most

What do more mature investors want?

Is it roller-coaster ride stocks? Fee-laden mutual funds? Paltry interest payments on bank CDs? Or secure investments where they will know what they're contractually expected to receive?

As I begin writing this book, the stock market, as measured by the Standard and Poor's 500 Index (S&P), has just broken another record high and the Dow Jones Industrial Average has surpassed the 20,000 mark. At the same time, many market indicators, including corporate returns and year-over-year sales of all U.S. goods and services (GDP), are way down. The market and the economy are at a huge disconnect. There are many reasons for this, and we will cover them in the coming chapters. We first need to understand the risks today's record-breaking stock market presents to everyone. Even more importantly, we need to understand what the market presents to investors who are either past or almost past their working years—investors who are reliant on their savings to carry them through the rest of their lives.

As a financial advisor serving the older, wealthier clients who make Central Florida their home, I'm trusted with tens of millions of dollars for clients of age and beyond. These are clients who never want me to call them to say, "You just lost 20 percent of your value in a correction, but stay the course anyway." And that's good, because I try to position them so I never have to make that painful call.

As today's stock market highs mathematically create more potential for loss, investors ought to consider making a paradigm shift away from traditional of "buy and hold" strategies and stock market outperformance.

This change in thinking is particularly true for more mature investors who don't have 7 to 10 years or more to wait out a large stock market drop—a drop that history suggests is all but certain.

For decades, professionals told investors that while stocks might be a little rocky from one day to the next, over the long run, they offer a return of 8 to 10 percent. Historically, there have been periods where this was true. There have also been periods where they crashed and were down, and only got back to their starting point after 16 years. This, I argue, makes holding a high percentage of stock market investments the wrong strategy for anyone who can't wait 16 years. What's worse is that the crawl back to the starting point, after more than a decade, is never certain and entails its own rocky path. It becomes even harder on the retiree if they use any of the investments to pay bills or to buy something. That would mean they now have less money available to grow when the market returns.

As Americans get older, they need to consider a paradigm shift to the type of investments that tend to not topple like stocks. Even younger Americans should make a paradigm shift, because the traditional thought is fraught with holes that could easily sink your portfolio.

The world has changed, unfortunately. Investments and stocks, during the first decade of the new millennium, reflected a changing investment climate. Here are five realities that now should be on the top of your list of considerations:

1. The financial crisis that started in 2008 kicked off unprecedented emergency measures that have a long-term depressive effect on growth.

2. High-speed trading and engineered financial tools throughout the world tend to enhance and multiply the risk of problems.

3. The nation is getting older. When Social Security first started, there were 42 workers paying in for each retiree. Today, only three workers support each retiree. With an aging population and longer life expectancy, one can only expect that the ratio will get worse.

4. The United States is no longer the undisputed center of the economic universe. Developing nations with lower wages and younger workers are creating increased levels of competition against American companies.

5. The Sandwich Generation* carries a particular burden, with their grown kids still living at home and their parents having moved in with them so they can get by on their budget. Three generations living under the same roof is becoming much more common than it was in recent history.

Your responsibility is to recognize these realities and not sit idly by.

---

* http://www.pewresearch.org/daily-number/the-sandwich-generation-burdens-on-middle-aged-americans-on-the-rise/

A SECURE RETIREMENT IS POSSIBLE— YOU JUST NEED TO ADJUST

As a financial advisor, I've made a concerted effort to make sure more people discover that Wall Street doesn't tell you everything. When you discover some of those things on your own, it changes the picture dramatically. There are investment options they don't want you to know about. Many of these are prudent solutions to the "five realities" described, but they aren't presented as methods to fulfill your investment goals because the professionals might earn less money than the stock market–based strategies. The media is a willing participant in keeping people in the dark as well. Advertising dollars are what keep them in business. If the advertisers are stock trading platforms, brokerage firms, and mutual fund companies, then these are the guests they bring on their shows. In my opinion, in many instances, the media doesn't even know there are better solutions. They get their information, in large part, from the Wall Street companies themselves. This is why what gets almost all the attention will continue to get all the airtime, advertising space, and articles written, even if it goes against the real purpose that retirees are invested.

What I tell people when I'm a guest on CNBC, Fox Business, or any of the top business shows, and when I'm at my public speaking engagements, is this: *You CAN help protect your money. You are NOT completely at the mercy of the financial markets and economic surprises.*

I'll explain that it's really not difficult for most people to grasp a better strategy. It's really more common sense than you might think. The best approach I find is to begin by asking:

- Do your investments suit your purpose?

- If they don't fit your purpose, are you open to shifting the way you think about investments?

If you are, then each of the chapters in this book will put you on a much more confident path to avoiding investment problems than anything I've found being taught anyplace else.

The first part of this book discusses ever-increasing dangers and how the old watchdogs are failing small investors. The second part discusses my own values and how to find the right investments without being encumbered by dangerous methodologies. The last section lays out timeless principles and the Truth (with a capital 'T") about how to always have the money you need in retirement. It's my hope that readers will experience an "aha!" moment as they visit each chapter. The "aha" moment is when you suddenly make the shift in thinking away from what Wall Street bombards you with, and toward what you need. Some people take longer than others, but, when you finally get it, the reaction—the *aha!*—will cause you to never think about your investments traditionally again. Investment expectations permanently shift, and you can begin investing with a more common sense approach that supports your financial goals.

In my advisory practice, this "aha" moment usually happens when someone attends one of my financial classes. There are hot buttons and trigger points that most people don't give much thought to until they learn about them and how they impact them directly. Often, they can't believe they took as long as they did to discover this knowledge. In my classes, I discuss what should be on their financial "front-burner" and why. They discover important elements to their financial security that they wish someone had told them about long ago. The next eight chapters will help you with these front-burner considerations and lead you to experience your own *aha!* moment.

I provide useful and valuable information to people because I find it deeply rewarding. People are often outwardly grateful that someone showed them strategies and concepts that will make a large impact on their lives. The comfort level I have with all of my clients is extremely high. When I explain the pitfalls of what others, including those on TV, have shown them, and the benefits of what I can do, it creates a sacred bond—a bond of honesty and trust that has them sending their good friends and close family to my office.

People who come to my office and my classes, and some who never do business with me, express how thankful they are for the "better" way of thinking and for pointing out areas that have been ignored for too long.

The concept is like being the Mother Teresa of the financial world and trying to do only good. It may sound silly, but when something becomes a *calling*, I want to show it to as many people as I possibly can and help them through their challenges, long-term. This creates a permanent solution.

So, I bet right about now you just want to skip to the last section on *Income Strategies to Last a Lifetime*. Trust me, the understanding will come quicker if you take this one chapter at a time. You may be wondering how it could be so easy, and if so, why doesn't everyone invest in his or her future this way? I admit, I do have an ulterior motive; it's to help people through education or directly as clients. Doing what is best for people who come to my office is my greatest reward.

WE'RE ALL SHAPED BY OUR EXPERIENCES

I grew up in a close family in Maryland. I'm the only boy of three children, and we are all near in age. In fact, Mom was bringing a new Eastham into the world every 13 months for 3 years. Helping each other made life easier, and coordinating everything from taking showers before school to whose turn it was to wash the dishes helped shape my being. I didn't grow up rich. We lived in a suburban community and were a middle-class family. My dad provided for the family as a computer programmer, and my mother was a stay-at-home mom for the majority of my school life. We had everything we needed, and we lived a comfortable life. My dad taught us about having a good work ethic by example. He didn't tell us we had to work hard; he just did it, and impressed upon us the importance of being well-educated not just from books, but from life.

I spent much of my childhood plugged into music, and I've always been a musician at heart. I played the drums in the marching band and naturally gravitated toward the drum set and rock 'n' roll. For a time, I felt certain I was headed toward a career as a professional musician. Music was always a main focus of mine growing up. In fact, I even started out in college as a music major. Obviously, I chose a different path, as market rhythms eventually became my passion.

They say that music is math, and at some point, the mathematical or, more specifically, the "common sense" portion of my brain realized that I should probably have a plan to fall back on beyond my musical inclination. I needed something I could count on for providing income, rather than hoping and praying that my music career would be successful. It was after a life-changing conversation with my dad that I began to add business courses the following semester. I quickly gravitated toward accounting. It might seem like a huge shift from drumming, but, instead of counting beats, I was counting "beans." The transition was actually quite easy for me. I graduated and began my career at a CPA firm almost immediately—not as exciting as the life of a rock star, but, it gave me a steady income. Consistent, reliable income is very enabling, and it helped me purchase the TAMA Superstar Series Drum Kit I had always dreamed of playing.

Today, reflecting on my childhood, I realize that I very much had a mindset of entitlement as a kid. I felt like I deserved a lot of good things, and I was lucky enough to have parents who provided a high level of comfort and compassion. This mindset changed quite suddenly, and although I did not enjoy it at the time, within what felt like a complete wreckage, I found my true self.

FINDING MY TRUE SELF

I was newly married, planning our family, and dreaming of all the possibilities in our future. Without warning or being married for even a year yet, I lost my job and didn't see it coming. I learned a very big, very important lesson along the way.

I wondered, "How could this injustice happen to me?" This was my first reaction. "I just got married, we were settling in, I left playing music to live this 'responsible' life. That was my mindset. I never thought it was ever going to be like this, and it was both scary and infuriating.

Thankfully, the responsibility of providing for a family lights a fire under you to find a solution in a way that living in a comfortable home with your parents never could. A light started to flicker in my head, and that light quickly became painfully bright, allowing me to see. It was hard to admit to myself that I was acting as though someone should be taking care of me and making sure bad things didn't happen. No one was there to make things better; it was up to me to help myself. This recognition of self-reliance brought a new understanding to my world. It was actually a blessing.

I understood that I had to go back to the basics. Rebuild my whole life in a way that recognized that I'm the one responsible for seizing my own opportunities. I reap the result of my own efforts. I had to take everything I'd learned and restart my journey in a positive way.

I decided to start doing the blocking and tackling required in life to get out there and figure out what I wanted, and then implement the steps it would require to get there. This was the lesson I needed to understand so I could commit to achievable goals. It was why I put so much emphasis—in both my life and my clients' accounts—into taking purposeful steps and leaving as little to chance as possible. I could sit here today and say I wish somebody had taught me all of this when I was in junior high school, high school, or even college. But after this, I've learned that some of life's lessons have to be experienced. If I had been told how to overcome this situation, me doing so would have been far less effective, or even completely ineffective.

I came to terms with the fact that it's my responsibility to gain the knowledge I need, and that's what really changed my thinking. Now, I am grateful to God I lost my job back then. It pushed me to be the self-reliant man I am today. It shaped every part of my business. It shaped what I do for others and how I want to offer services that best fit their purposes, rather than just doing what everyone else is doing. I have too much regard for planning and executing to blindly follow models created under different circumstances. Every working day of the week, I offer facts and statistics that Wall Street powerhouses and the financial "talking heads" don't want you to hear.

When you find something that is better than other strategies and that truly benefits people, share it. I learned while growing up that helping others is always fulfilling. Be passionate, and establish your business in a way that you are the best you can be. Then, continue to refine it for as long as you are helping others. I have a purpose-driven life philosophy and a purpose-driven business model to help my clients get to where they need to go. I have a contract, or "covenant" if you will, with my clients. I will seek the best answers for their purposes and make sure the road they take is as smooth as possible.

WHY BECOMING A FINANCIAL ADVISOR DEALING IN INVESTMENTS WAS A BETTER PATH

I worked at a CPA firm in public accounting in my early years, primarily in audits and consulting, and I enjoyed being involved with corporate executives and entrepreneurs. I gained a lot of experience and knowledge by seeing how people were able to start businesses and make them work.

While there, I learned there was a need for financial advisory services and I passed the test for a securities license (Series 7) in 1987.

That environment created a natural interest in self-employment to some degree, and more so in doing things on my own terms so I could make more room for what I was passionate about, like writing and teaching.

Early on it was taboo in the CPA world to mix CPA work with financial planning and investing. I had a real interest in finance and the stock market, so I started talking to one of the firm partners about it, and the idea was immediately rejected.

However, as years went on, I actually transitioned to the corporate side of the business. I had some corporate positions as a financial executive, but as often happens in the profession, I decided I needed to become independent in order to accomplish what my heart told me was right. There is no such thing as the perfect time, so I weighed all my options and quickly implemented my plan. I left everything I knew, and the stability that went along with that life, for the opportunity to build the life I enjoy today as the owner of my own successful firm. I can honestly say, I don't regret anything that followed.

MY LIFE TODAY IS NOTHING SHORT OF A BLESSING

Today, thank God, both my parents are still alive and still married—going on 56 years now. They couldn't be happier with their 12 grandchildren between my sisters and me. My children are 22, 21, 16 and 9. They keep us very busy, and we are extremely grateful to be parents of such great kids.

My biggest fear for my children, when I look at today's mounting problems, is the economy. We all live in the shadow of $20 trillion of federal debt. That's an unfathomable number. It will continue to weigh heavily on the economy, and yet, few people want to take action to begin to fix the problem.

I try to teach my kids the things that I had to learn the hard way. Parents are the primary teachers for their kids, but there is only so much coaching and parenting you can do. There are some obstacles they have to figure out on their own, many of which were never anticipated by the teacher. You teach the foundational things like integrity, character, humility, discipline, and self-reliance, to name a few. You show them you have to be willing to do the hard thing when your mind or body doesn't want you to.

Perseverance is something you learn when you learn a musical instrument, a sport, a profession or anything that must be *mastered*. It's the same with your financial life. In my case, I had to keep practicing the drums, even when my arms hurt or my fingers had blisters. Success didn't come easily but the journey was well worth it. Even after all the effort to execute my plan to be a musician, I had to make sure I had a plan B. Today, I talk to my kids about the importance of having their plan B and helping you find yours is a big reason I wrote this book.

I realize that with kids, there's a small window of time to influence them and to help them find answers to tough questions before they start doing their own thing, where Mom and Dad aren't part

The Eastham Family

Michael with his first love, drumming.

of their lives on that level anymore. That's one of the things that drove me to focus hard on helping them understand what the important things were in life and how they factored into the quality of life they would live. You have to decide who you are, determine what you want, and make a plan to accomplish those dreams. What are the things in your life that are non-negotiable?

A LIFE WORTHY OF BEING REPLICATED

There are multiple reasons why I wrote this book for you. The primary driving force was that there weren't enough people teaching this investment philosophy. Yet, I've seen it not only transform my own financial future, but also impact many others in a positive way. I've focused on developing it over the last several years, but in reality, it's been cultivated over the course of my entire life. I know it's powerful and it works, so how can I not share it with everyone who will listen?

· 2 ·

Fact-Checking Wall Street

About 20 minutes southwest of my office is a place many consider to be the greatest theme park in the world. Disney World attracts about 47 million people each year who travel to Lake Buena Vista to visit Mickey Mouse.

Mickey is the recognized symbol of this land of magic and make-believe, and people expect that when they enter the park they'll be swept away to fantasy land. That experience may include roller-coaster rides, odd characters, fake castles, flying elephants, trips through Tomorrowland, and a large magical kingdom where happiness abounds. But I'm sure almost everyone entering Disney knows it's make-believe.

Wall Street—and by Wall Street I mean the broader providers of investments, securities, and mutual funds (not just New York)— also has a recognized animal symbol. Appropriately enough, that symbol is a bull. The Wall Street experience can suspend reality for its visitors as it tries to sweep you off to its own fantasy land of consistent double-digit growth. Often, in the case of Wall Street, that might result in putting your investments on a roller-coaster ride and charging you a hefty price for admission. Once people understand how all the characters interact with the public and each other, I find they never look at Wall Street the same way.

Wall Street has a specific business model. Not unlike any other industries, decisions are driven by profit.

Imagine that you're the CEO of one of the big Wall Street firms. As CEO, what's your objective? Is it to make sure the customer has the lowest price and best product, or is it to make sure you return as much money as possible to the "bottom line?" The CEO has a fiduciary responsibility to shareholders and cares about doing what's best for the customer only to the extent that it provides maximum shareholder value. If they behaved any other way, they would not be acting in accordance with their position.

So, in that position, let's say there are two different investment options to sell to the public. The first is extremely profitable for the company. The second is less profitable to the firm, but provides a better outcome for the customer. Which of the two is the company going to try to promote and distribute most broadly? In the interest of the stockholders, more marketing energy will be put behind the most profitable option for the firm, even though it is the less desirable for you, the consumer. If you, as CEO, acted in any other way, your bonus could be slashed or you could be terminated. Earning the most for the owners (shareholders) is, after all, your responsibility.

So, the marching orders from the top ranks of most large Wall Street firms is obviously "earn the most profit." You see, there is an inherent conflict of interest that exists here that does not bother you if you are buying soap or toilet paper, but it really makes you mad when it has to do with your finances. In other words, your interests are more in sync with the CEO's if you own the stock of the Wall Street firm than if you have a brokerage account there. This goal enters into the company culture and everything they develop or recommend. For instance, take the staff in the research department; they know to look through the more profitable offerings to find recommendations. They may not ever bother researching the least profitable, even if it better serves clients. Branch managers are under the same mindset. They are not only aware of the corporate objectives, but their income—including bonuses—that could vary widely based on maximizing profits.

That is the overall dynamic of a large Wall Street firm, it has far-reaching effects on other related businesses. Since we are talking about Wall Street in the broadest of terms, let's look at how your neighborhood financial advisor might be affected. It's rare for a local advisor to have an independent research department. The research they rely on is often adopted from the major firms that we identified at the top of the chain, so their advice and information actually is also disseminated down through smaller, local firms as well. As mentioned, these recommendations are often skewed by the "big guys" and their own profit motives.

And it goes further. The same biased Wall Street information is also disseminated to the people we all rely on for information: the news. Imagine you're a reporter for the financial media. It doesn't matter if it's print or broadcast, your background is likely to be in journalism or other writing. Most reporters of financial news are not analysts and have no background in analysis. If they were analysts, that would be a full-time job by itself. They wouldn't have time to also do the job as a writer or reporter. In fact, many aren't hired because of their investment knowledge; they are hired because they can write. You'd be surprised at how many writers were at one time employed as, let's say, science writers one year, sports the next, and then they'd find their way into writing for a financial outlet. Don't expect them to be experts at anything but writing.

Here is what you should expect from the media. The company they work for is also focused on bottom-line profit. This comes in the form of advertising dollars. Rather than doing raw research, media outlets will interview spokesmen from the firms that advertise with them or ones they would like to have advertise with them.

It makes sense for them on many fronts. For one, it allows them to be a little lazy, because it's easier. This allows them to satisfy the constant hunger for 24-hour news, and, over time, it will especially help their advertising profit.

When they interview an advertiser or potential advertiser as a news story, the person being interviewed is often in the driver's seat because the news outlet has a profit motive. This allows them to publicly hawk, under the guise of financial news, whatever message or product is best (most profitable) for their firm. If this doesn't sound probable, think about it in reverse. What if your TV station or magazine reported something that made it more difficult for your advertiser to sell their products? It's likely that your advertisers would begin to reallocate marketing dollars to other venues.

It's business as usual and you must, as an investor, be aware of it. The media is just making a good business decision based on profit to take story shortcuts and maximize their profit stream. The stories they are reporting are the stories that the big Wall Street firms want told. They are telling you what they want you to hear because it is most profitable to them. Even if facts are checked, the expertise of the journalist may be insufficient to determine if the advice is bona fide.

To make matters worse, there are very few competing firms for news. In fact, 90 percent of all traditional media outlets are owned by only six companies.

The long tentacles of the mega Wall Street firms also infect other important institutions. Unfortunately, the educational outlets that teach investments are also tainted. As a CPA, I have a habit of immediately crunching numbers for my own determination of value. Even when I get to this point, I'm not finished. I have to run my results through another filter. That filter is the more

COMPANIES THAT OWN MEDIA OUTLETS

Major Holdings of the Six Conglomerates

GE	NEWSCORP	DISNEY	VIACOM	TIME WARNER	CBS
COMCAST	FOX	ABC	MTV	CNN	SHOWTIME
NBC	WALL STREET JOURNAL	ESPN	NICK JR.	HBO	SMITHSONIAN CHANNEL
UNIVERSAL PICTURES		PIXAR	BET	TIME	NFL.COM
FOCUS FEATURES	NEW YORK POST	MIRAMAX	CMT	WARNER BROTHERS	JEOPARDY
		MARVEL STUDIOS	PARAMOUNT PICTURES		60 MINUTES

Six conglomerates own 90 percent of all traditional media outlets.

Source: http://www.businessinsider.com/these-6-corporations-control-90-of-the-media-in-america-2012-6

emotion-driven, financial market reality filter. It took me a little while to understand that the human factor of emotions often makes the math involved inconsequential. I learned this as I was earning my Financial Industry Regulatory Authority (FINRA) registrations and immersing myself in investment and market analysis and strategies. What people experience in real life is quite a bit different from the expectations based on the math and logic in the classroom. It's important to study how markets have behaved historically under certain situations to do the complete analysis.

This is because the markets, in actual ebb and flow, are very often fueled by human emotion. When the strategies and truisms being taught are back-tested, over time, they tend to fit the advice being given. However, when investors need reliable guides on what to do in certain situations, the math and rules go out the window. They offer no protection at all because under extreme conditions (the most profitable or costly), the market loses all rationality. Emotions take over. This emotional effect occurs in both directions. It has driven markets up well beyond what schools teach as reasonable valuation, and they go down in the same way. In fact, emotions have caused markets to come crashing down to prices below where every investor using conventional teaching would be scooping up shares. And yet, they're still selling at that point.

There's a reason I believe the schools are still teaching financial advisors analytical techniques including ratios, valuation methodologies, diversification strategies, and holding periods: The entities that finance, provide material, or otherwise own the educational material are linked to Wall Street firms. It's often (not always) in the best interest of these big firms to provide information to advisors that help them maximize their profit. As a result, reality and common sense are often lacking in financial education.

The small investor is confronted with another confusing ploy. With every long-term run-up I've seen in stocks, as soon as people begin to question how long the bull market can last, the experts from large Wall Street firms show up on TV singing a tune that has been used through the ages. As investors begin to question whether the market can sustain its high level, the so-called experts, or hired voices from Wall Street, suddenly appear all over the news to calm them by saying, "This time, it's going to be different." They try to explain why the overvaluation of stocks using traditional benchmarks is not applicable in this case. They suggest "new realities" that never existed during other periods in history. "This time, it's going to be different," to my knowledge, has never held—not in the period leading up to the years 1899, 1929, 1966 and 2000.

The stock market cannot continue to go up indefinitely, as we'll confirm in later chapters. There is a rhythm to market moves that history has validated time and time again. When you hear someone representing Wall Street say those seven words, common sense suggests that we ignore them.

The dissemination of information from the large Wall Street firms actually influences smaller money managers. It creates bias in media reporting, and it creates partial financial education. Then, when investors might think about taking some money out of the market, highly paid "experts" tell them, "This time, it's going to be different." This all causes average investors to believe the bias and limit their own options to only those they are being bombarded with. The universe of investments, including those that may better suit their investing purposes, is significantly broader. Most of them just don't compete well for airtime or print.

In fact, the average investor at home who watches the business channel and reads the financial news in magazines is only getting a small glimpse of the picture. They aren't learning what they need to about market cycles, and they aren't even aware of what their investment options are. All along, they are only seeing what the large firms want them to see, because that is what those firms make the most money with. Small investors are being steered and may even believe that their only choices are stocks and mutual funds. The reality is, it simply isn't true.

OTHER DANGERS POSED BY WALL STREET

When it comes to larger firms, there is a cold disconnect between the firm they are dealing with and themselves. I believe this creates an environment less conducive to fair play. The person creating the investment, the seller, and the investor are all faceless. They don't interact in any way where the familiarity of a handshake and direct eye contact breeds more honest transactions. Once the face has been taken out of the various parties in a transaction, it's easier to sell a more profitable product, even if it isn't the best fit. The inside circles of Wall Street call this "increasing the return to broker." Faceless transactions make you, the investor, just a number, and it's much easier to fleece a number.

When you're sitting across from and looking into the eyes of your financial advisor, the recommendations, as far as I can tell, improve. I suggest you deal with local people you know. You're more likely to get a fair shake from Main Street (part of your community) than Wall Street. But still, be very selective when choosing a Main Street advisor.

ALL ADVISORS ARE NOT THE SAME

Just like any industry, there are some bad apples in the investment advisory business. Very often, it isn't even their fault. What's crucial for you is to make sure your advisor is competent. (We will discuss vetting an advisor in the second section of this book.)

Financial advisors are not always given the right tools. As you'll see, many advisors have their clients' best interests at heart but, that may not be enough. Their education and mentoring may not have been at firms that serve the client first. Most financial advisors either work for a large firm or get their start at a larger firm before starting their own advisory practice. The large firms invest a great deal of money to recruit and train new advisors. The training is twofold. It helps the new advisors obtain the proper registrations or licenses, and it teaches the selling culture of that firm. The dropout rate is high—somewhere around 91 percent. These firms know before they bring anyone onboard, they'll lose about 9 out of 10 trainees. Out of those who remain, it only takes one to do so well, that they more than cover the training cost of all those who didn't work out.

To increase the likelihood of finding someone who succeeds, firms usually don't screen for recruits with the most investment knowledge. They may not even pay any attention to integrity or to applicants with the intelligence to become great investors. What most large Wall Street firms seek is aggressiveness. For many of these firms, the ideal candidate is a twentysomething who wants to buy expensive toys. They look for a "stop-at-nothing" attitude and a person with a long list of wealthy connections, including family and friends they aren't afraid to call. More than anything, they want someone who will do as they're told and adopt the culture and process as it is spoon-fed to them. A very high percentage of financial planners began at one of these firms. They were trained to be aggressive salespeople, not to have investment smarts. If this doesn't sound like a recipe for informed advice, you're right. We'll learn how to check your advisor's background later on.

Most advisors actually get their education from the same places consumers do—TV, magazines, and newspapers. So, they repeat the same advice that they've gotten from the news, which is the same narrative that the advertisers ingrain into the public's head, the axioms of "buy and hold":

"It's not about timing the market, it's about time IN the market."

"60/40 diversification based on the rule of 100*."

These axioms are often taught as if they are reality, so Wall Street repeats it from so many places that they don't question whether it's great advice. It's just accepted as conventional wisdom.

These axioms are, in themselves, part of the problem and should be fact-checked. Here's one worth expounding upon: "Buy and hold" is touted by Wall Street as the best way to invest. They say you won't miss the good days if you stay in for the long term. This is overheard so often that most accept it as fact and don't question

---

* http://www.investopedia.com/articles/financial-advisors/011916/why-604 0-portfolio-no-longer-good-enough.asp?lgl=bt1tn-above-textnote

it. The reasoning given since 2008, when market participants were very fearful, has been, "You don't want to miss the 10 best days." The large Wall Street firms and their public relations departments found this was a way to keep you invested. They turned fear of investing into "there is a cost to succumbing to fear." Unfortunately for investors who believed them, this only placed half the data into view. When all the details are viewed, the message is literally the reverse of the truth. It proves that there is a cost to succumbing to the public relations spin disseminated by Wall Street. After all, they get paid when you're invested, not when you're on the sidelines. This demonstrates once again that you can't rely on what you hear or read. It's important to fact-check on your own or find an advisor you trust—someone you trust with literally almost everything you own.

Alternatively, what they didn't tell you is how well off you would be if you missed the 10 worst days. Using their own logic, this would cause you not to "buy and hold," but instead to trade the market. If you were to have missed the 10 best days each year since 1928, an investment of a dollar would have grown to $23.62 in 2011. If you missed the 10 worst days over that same period, you'd be almost 10 times better off than if you had missed the 10 best days. That's not where the fact-checking stops, because if you had missed the 10 best along with the 10 worst over that period, you'd still be three times better off than if you had missed the 10 best. But, they still tell you to "buy and hold," and it sounds logical. It certainly serves Wall Street's profit motives, but it may not serve yours.

WALL STREET'S "MARKETING AGENT"—THE MEDIA

As further evidence that the media is not the best place to get your news, I'll highlight actual examples of their dismal track record:

- On March 11, 1996, the cover of *U.S. News and World Report* blared "Investors Beware!" But, from March 11, 1996 to the end of that year, the Dow gained about 17.3 percent. The following year it gained 22.8 percent.

- In August 1997, while the market was rising by 19.4 percent, *Money* magazine insisted you "Sell Stock Now!" However, the Dow rose for the next two years; 15.3 percent in 1998, and 25.2 percent in 1999.

- *Fortune* magazine felt so sure the market was going to "CRASH" that it warned you on September 28, 1998 in big red letters. As it turned out, the market did not crash—in fact, prices continued to rise until April of 2000.

- From April 11, 2000 until October 9, 2002, the stock market had finally fallen. The decline was the first wave down after the "Goldilocks'" economy, and it took a 35.4 percent chunk out of the Dow.

---

* http://www.investopedia.com/terms/g/goldilockseconomy.asp

■ The "Money" section of *USA Today* on October 2, 2002 wrote about the decline, telling readers there was "No end in sight. . . ." In hindsight, the experts from *USA Today* could not have been more wrong. On October 10, 2002, the stock market began heading back up.

It's important to note that it's not only the "trusted experts" in the print media who get it so wrong. There are many popular financial TV shows that are created more for entertainment than sound financial advice with their sound effects, bells, whistles and loud monologues about individual stocks. *Barron's* did a study of those recommendations before the 2008 financial meltdown. *Barron's* is a high-caliber weekly financial news publication. They looked at Jim Cramer's recommendations in 2006 and 2007 and concluded that his picks gained an average of 12 percent. They also found that, for the exact same period studied, the S&P gained an additional 10 percent for a total of 22 percent. Cramer was about half as good as just passively investing in the index.

Jim Cramer and others have a huge following. Television personalities report with confidence and develop a flock who seem genuinely star-struck. What's remarkable is that the followers repeat what they've heard their favorite TV star "stock guesser" say. They tell it to friends as though it's preordained. A quick Google search of each of these stock market spokesmen will unveil an uncanny ability for them to be exactly wrong. They keep their jobs because people watch, not because they have accurate insights or forecasts.

Meanwhile, there are people who successfully manage the billions of investment dollars for Wall Street firms, banks, insurance companies, and corporations. These hidden stars don't publicly discuss their successful investment methods outside of their quiet circle. We'll get to their methods and how to implement them for your own household in the last section of the book. It is important to first lay the groundwork in order for you to get the most out of my common sense approach and the other discoveries you will find as you read my book.

• 3 •

Stock Market History

". . . the one thing they (my clients) all agree on, is that history tends to repeat itself."

As you may recall, at the outset (in Chapter 1) I said that as a financial advisor, I make every effort to make sure more people discover that "Wall Street doesn't tell you everything." There will be several ideas and realities in this chapter that are very important to investors everywhere, yet Wall Street firms, although they use this information themselves, have no incentive to share it.

In my discussions with clients, it's clear that people, even in the same age group and from the same community, have a very broad array of different views and ideas on topics such as the best way to spend free time, political leanings, child-rearing, religious beliefs, etc. The one thing their years of experience has taught them—the one thing they all agree on—is that history tends to repeat itself. I think as we get older, we see more and more that it does, so this is no longer merely a concept; we take it as a reality.

In fact, my close friend and business associate is host of the Newsmax TV show *The Income Generation with David J. Scranton.* Dave has had Steve Forbes on as a guest, and I heard Forbes describe the phenomenon this way: "History is people. While times and circumstances change, human nature does not." It's human activity that drives human circumstances. Economic change and market price movement is the result of human input. This input includes emotions such as fear and characteristics like greed, and it's also dependent on perception of value at any given moment. Price movements in any market are determined by supply and demand factors.

In this chapter, I'm discussing overall stock market dynamics, although the concepts can easily be applied to individual corporate shares.

Supply, when we're talking about the stock market, is the amount of stock offered for sale at a given time. The number of available shares for sale can increase or decrease based on changes in competing investments, such as interest being paid on bonds. If interest rates go up, typically some investors will move money from stocks to bonds. The effect is that alternative or competing investments will affect the amount of supply available for investors. There could also be other reasons for increased or decreased supply of stock offered for sale. If future expectations change, the number of sellers will change. The absolute number of shares in existence also changes as new shares enter the market. One common way this happens is with an increase in public offerings of new stock, which increases shares available. As I'll explain in Chapter 4, shares can be taken out of the market, which reduces supply and puts upward pressure on prices. Relatively speaking, the supply of stock does not change dramatically and is much less of a factor in price changes than demand.

Demand for stock can and does fluctuate dramatically, even within the day. The reasons include economic reports that are released, which cause investors to either view future earnings for better or for the worse; demand from overseas, depending on the economic climate shifts away from home; and lower interest rates increasing demand, which would place upward pressure on stocks.

Small investors do not often consider it this way, but the markets are a culmination of human activity and human decision making. And, as mentioned earlier, human nature does not change over time.

EQUILIBRIUM BETWEEN PRICE, SUPPLY AND DEMAND

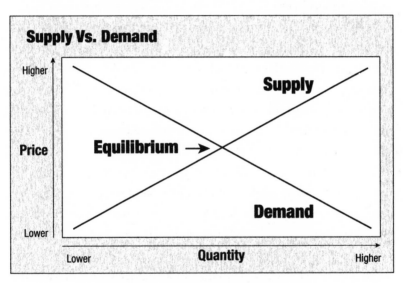

How Price is Determined by the Populace.
Picture the demand curve moving higher. The price would rise as supply increases to meet that demand. As quantity rises, the supply curve moves to the right and prices fall.

This is an author creation; investopedia was used as a source: http://www.investopedia.com/university/economics/economics3.asp

The chart above shows how prices are determined in a free market. If the demand curve should rise, prices will rise along the demand curve to reach equilibrium (and vice versa). If supply (quantity)

should increase, the supply curve will intersect with the demand curve at lower prices (and vice versa). The graph demonstrates how market incentives affect each other to determine price levels.

AVERAGE HISTORICAL RETURN OF STOCKS

When my kids were younger, I was extremely involved in every aspect of youth soccer. At the end of each season all the players and their parents would get together to honor teams that had the best record or were standouts in other ways. The unfortunate reality about statistics: Whether they are team stats or any other category, they can often be used to tell completely different stories. As a CPA I tend to take a 360-degree view each time I look at numbers used to measure success or failure. One year, I came across such peculiar stats on one of the soccer teams that I wasn't sure whether they deserved to be honored. The team's statistics were so contradictory that I sometimes use the story when discussing the success and failure of the stock market.

When six to seven-year-olds play soccer, the teams average between four to five goals per game. I always kept track of statistics and other key numbers for the league. One year, one of the teams had scored an average of 6.2 goals per game. This was far more than the average for all the other teams combined, which was 4.4 goals per game. On the surface, you would think that they must have dominated the field that year. One would think they must have had a winning season and that they probably came in first.

Well, the truth was anything but evident from these numbers. The team that averaged 6.2 goals per game had actually come in dead last out of the eight teams in the league. In fact, every other team in the league had a better record. How can that be? After all, they scored more goals throughout the season than any other team. Well, as I mentioned, statistics can be deceiving. Here's what happened: During the full season, the team was not very good at scoring points. In their very first game, they scored 27 goals against the opposing team. The final score was 27 to 4. I wasn't at the game, so I don't know the reason, but for the remainder of the season, the same team rarely scored more than 3 points in a game. They had the worst record of the league, but the highest amount of points scored, which, when divided into the number of games, gave them the highest average.

I relay this story occasionally to clients who come to my office—especially those who tell me the stock market returns on average 10 percent—then ask if they should be invested in stocks. Not unlike the soccer team with the highest average, the truth is, by at least one measure, the stock market does return 10 percent. By other measures, 12 percent, and by others, as low as 7 percent. These numbers are averages, and they're taken over time. It's not a set return that you earn each year, just as 6.2 goals is not what the soccer team scored each game. There were at least three games where the team did not score at all. In fact, they only won two games that season. Despite the proclaimed statistical average returns of stock market, many retirees find they lost their whole "retirement season" waiting for that one big game to pull them through.

BULL AND BEAR CYCLES

The idea that history repeats itself is evident in the chart on the next page, of the Dow Jones Industrial Average for the period 1966 to 1982.

The patterns on this graph are actual stock market movements that occurred during this period. Stock prices may appear random, but there are repeating price cycles that are clear when charted. The cycles, which are driven by the total of market supply and investor demand, build and wane in a way that creates price trends. Over very long periods of time, the investor who has stayed invested has earned an average return of between 7 and 12 percent.

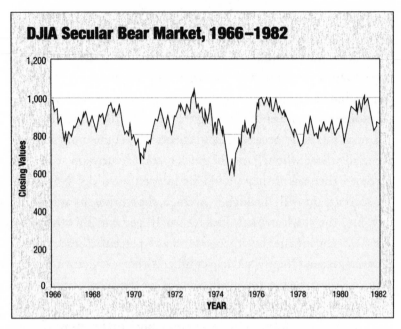

After 16 years, The Percentage of Growth in Stocks was Zero.
Although there may be Bullish and Bearish periods within a Secular
Bear Market, over time investors may not gain at all.

Source Data: https://measuringworth.com/DJA/result.php

In the chart, you'll notice that during this particular 16-year period, the return to the investor of Dow stocks was close to zero
percent. In other words, individuals who retired at the beginning
of this period at age 65, fully invested in stocks, found themselves
at age 81 with no investment growth.

The reason is that the cycles you see in the chart are viewed as
shorter cycles within a long-term or "secular" bear market cycle.
There are bull and bear periods within a secular cycle, just as a
child with a fever may experience his temperature dropping, only
for it to spike back up. He may occasionally rally and appear

better, but it doesn't mean he's cured. These secular bear market cycles can last around 20 years, sometimes a little shorter, and others a little longer.

Wall Street and the media that provides the public with news and ideas prefer to speak about the shorter cycles. However, investors near or in retirement should pay most of their attention to longer cycles that may keep their money on a roller-coaster ride for a long period—a roller-coaster that never provides the average growth they were looking for and, as we'll see, may take them for 30 percent or more without warning. Well, almost without a warning.

HERE'S YOUR WARNING

Stocks and ownership in companies have been trading on the New York Stock Exchange for more than 200 years. That's a very long history from which a numbers person, like myself, can derive information about what has happened in the past. Although, as they say, this is no guarantee of future direction, I'll presume that spring will always follow winter, and summer will always follow spring. Some years, spring weather will start a little behind the calendar, and other years it will come early, but we're all confident enough in the patterns to act on them. We put away our winter clothes and schedule more outdoor activities as we move past late March. We don't bet against it. When we look at the much longer history of stocks than is often presented to investors, we'd also be reluctant, to say the least, to bet against it.

Unfortunately, any longer history is very difficult to find. Most often, TV reports on how the market is doing in the current year. Top sites on the internet aren't much better. If you try to generate a long-term chart on Yahoo Finance, you'll find it difficult if not impossible to go back beyond 10 years. Bloomberg, CNN, Money, and even CNBC Online will take you back only five years. That isn't enough information on which to draw any kind of trend conclusion when secular cycles can last 20 years or more. The best of the bunch is probably Google Finance. If you draw a stock chart on Google Finance and hit "MAX," it will draw a chart with 40 years of history. That's still only the late 1970s, and it does not include enough visual data for anyone to see where we are in the longer secular cycle. It's the secular cycle that a retiree expecting to live up to 20 or 30 years longer should consider.

If you only consider a chart that goes back five or 10 years, you will see a chart of a market that has a mostly upward slope. If you go back 40 years, you'll get the same impression. It's easy to view the stock market as something that only keeps growing. I won't accuse the information source as intentionally setting a positive

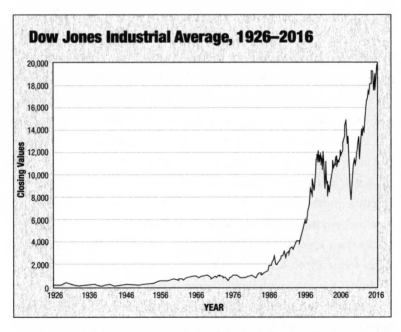

The Famous Mountain Chart – Seeing is not believing. Brokers show this chart to their clients in order to hype a market which is far more up and down than indicated in this long period.

Source Data: https://measuringworth.com/DJA/result.php

bias toward stocks, as much as I will point out that there is a precedent for providing only partial information to the small investor.

In the 1990s, when the internet was foreign to most and only very slow dial-up was available, investment brokers kept a chart handy or posted it up on their wall. It portrayed a very carefully selected set of data points. It was dubbed the "mountain chart" because of its shape. This chart only covered the period from 1926 to 1996. The brokers' apparent intention was to get investors caught up in the hype of the massive increase the chart appeared to demonstrate. Not highlighted were the ups and downs along the way. Even this chart demonstrates that the longer trends are 35-year cycles. That is to say, if you invested at the wrong time, you may sit at a financial loss or, at best, have missed out on other opportunities. There's a very good chance you may have to wait years to see any growth in your portfolio.

This manipulation of trusting people frustrates me, and frankly, it's one of the reasons I teach classes, make national TV and radio appearances, host my own radio show and ultimately, what encouraged me to write this book.

U.S. STOCK MARKET, THE DISMAL YEARS

I don't have to stretch your memory too far back to highlight some very dismal years for investors. They were particularly bad for retirees who planned on "average" returns for stocks. The 10-year period ending in 2009 was one of those periods. If you had a retirement account invested to earn the average of the New York Stock Exchange during this period, you would have lost, on average, 0.5 percent per year during that calendar decade. What's even worse is that when inflation is taken into consideration, the buying power of the retirees' stocks would have declined 3.3

percent per year on average. Many who expected to retire at the beginning of the new millennium postponed their plans, and others who were in retirement postponed plans for vacation and other nonessential purchases.

If we travel back a bit further to the decade of the 1970s, the market, as measured by the S&P 500, lost buying power of 1.4 percent per year when accounting for inflation. As for non-decade 10-year periods, those ending in 1937 and 1938 were much worse than the 1970s or 2000s. Fortunately, not as many people invested in stocks back then.*

The first decade of the millennium was particularly devastating to households. During the 1980s, mutual funds had become a popular way for the average person to have diversified stock market exposure. The cyclical bull market that began in the late 1980s saw even higher gains during the 1990s. The 17 percent average gain in stocks during the 1990s made it the second-most lucrative decade (after the 1950s) for stock market investors. The period saw a growth in discount brokers, which allowed small investors to stock-pick for minimal charges, and stock mutual funds were considered the conservative investment. With the general mindset that stocks only go up and 17 percent returns were normal, many retirees entered year 2000 fully invested in the stock market.

WHAT HISTORY SUGGESTS IN THE COMING YEARS

An accepted definition of "secular bear market" is an extended period when the stock market has risen and fallen. At the end of the period, historically lasting 15 to 20 years, the market is left with growth approximating zero percent. This investor roller-coaster

* Source: http://www.wsj.com/articles/SB10001424052748704786204574607993448916718

ride historically includes at least three large drops and many smaller ups and downs in between.

Extended Periods of Zero Percent and Above-Average Stock Market Growth

The diagram here illustrates that although stocks return around 10 percent on average a year, secular bear market cycles have prevented many "buy and hold" investors from experiencing any growth at all during bear markets, which have lasted as long as 25 years. That's a lifetime for someone retiring today who is planning on growth in their retirement account to provide for some of their needs over a couple of decades or more. It doesn't even keep up with inflation, so it is actually worth less to them despite the risks taken investing the savings.

If, for example, we looked at the period from 1899 to 1921, "buy and hold" investors had more than two decades with no growth. This was followed by eight years of strong price growth

10% Average Annual Return
2% to 3% Dividends + 7% to 8% Growth

BEAR MARKET	BULL MARKET
P/E 30+, 0% Growth	P/E 6–8, 12-15% Growth
1900–1921	1921–1929
1929–1954	1954–1966
1966–1982	1982–2000
2000–????	

The Investor Roller-Coaster Ride by Period. The often quoted 10% average returns includes up to 3% dividends and long bearish periods offsetting the bullish periods.

from 1921 to 1929. The market crash, which helped cause the Great Depression, occurred in 1929 and left investors who held on waiting until 1954 to break even at around zero percent. After 1954, stock prices picked up and served anyone invested for the 12-year period ending in 1966 quite well. Most of my clients have some memory of the stock market from 1966 to 1982 as a dangerous place to invest, and judging by the zero percent growth investors received, they are correct. The period following 1982 and ending in 2000 is the period that has shaped my clients' and many Baby Boomers' paradigms on stocks. This was a very profitable period with stocks consistently returning well above average returns and with participation in the investment markets reaching new highs.

Another important piece of information we can learn from this graphic is that the price-earnings ratio (P/E) of the market can be used to determine the next direction. Understanding what P/E measures is relatively simple. The P/E ratio of a stock is a method investors use to determine a stock's value. As it's used in the graphic (and for the remainder of the book), I'm quoting the average of the overall stock market. To understand P/E, I'll explain how it would work in a rental property. If an investor bought a house at a price of $120,000 and in renting it collected $1,000 a month, they collect $12,000 per year. It would take 10 years to cover the initial cost of the home. The house has a P/E ratio of 10. If that same house costs the investor/landlord $360,000, and they still collect only $1,000 a month, it would take 30 years to cover the purchase price. The house has a P/E of 30. This measuring tool is used extensively to find value in stocks.

Viewing the P/E ratio adds further historical detail to help determine the next direction of the market. As touched on previously, each time a secular bull market cycle has exhausted itself—1929, 1966, 1999–2000—P/E ratios have been near or above 30. This is a warning sign that one ignores at their own peril.

The number 30 seems to be when market players stop chasing and decide that they would be overpaying if they kept buying. It's where many decide to take profits, which causes the market to stall, if not fall.

On the secular bear market cycle side, use P/E ratios as a forecasting tool to determine if it has reached its conclusion. Typically, as the end of a secular bear market approaches, P/E ratios fall below 10, very often to between a P/E of 6 to 8. At 10, stocks are a third of what they were at 30. At 6 to 8, bears seem to wake up and decide that they want to be bulls for a while.

We are currently in the 20-year period since the last bull market, and it has all the attributes of a classic secular bear market. The future is never certain, but we can be certain of this: There are only three things the market can do. It can go up, it can move down, or it can continue to move sideways.

UP, DOWN, OR SIDEWAYS?

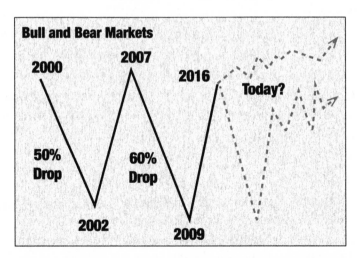

The Historic Pattern that You Should Not Bet Against. Through 2016 the market has not yet started on it's typical path downward because of the government stimulus. That period we're told is drawing to a close. Will the market resume it's downward historic pattern?

We've established that the average bull or bear market cycle is 15 to 20 years; this adds to 30 or up to 40 years for the market to go full cycle. As I mentioned earlier, the secular bear investor roller-coaster ride historically includes at least three large drops and many smaller ups and downs in between. So, the question now is one of probabilities. Will the market ignore history and keep rising past the 20-year period starting in 2000? Or is it much more probable that the next three years include a period where stocks again fall 20 to 50 percent and take an extended period of years to recover?

Don't place your bets yet, because there is a bit more information I haven't covered yet. In February 2013, stocks did reach a level slightly higher than their highs in 2000 and 2007. This, some would argue, broke the pattern. The market broke new highs again immediately after election day, as the market breathed a sigh of relief knowing the election had been settled one way or the other (the markets dislike uncertainty, so a Mitt Romney win may have also caused a relief rally). I'd argue that both events are special circumstances that don't change the overall pattern. In fact, in 2013, the government was throwing an unprecedented amount of stimulus into the economy; this level was unsustainable, borrowed from future years, and since late 2014, as we'll discuss in Chapter 4, is being removed very slowly.

Based on all these conditions, I tell my clients that the probable direction of stocks from here is dramatically down. And, based on history, investors will take years to recover.

My reasoning is primarily based on these three details, supported by history:

1. If a new market cycle began in 2013, it would be the *first time* in its history that the market recovered from a secular bear market in only 13 years.

2. If we have a complete and permanent recovery from 2000 without three large drops, it would also be the *first time* this happened.

3. If we experience a full recovery before another huge drop, it would be the *first time* the markets acted this way while the P/E ratio is not below 10 percent. The S&P 500 is currently above 24 percent.

How likely is it that we have three "first-time ever" situations in history? Anything can happen, after all the Chicago Cubs won the world series after more than 100 years; but when your future depends on being right, my advice is: Don't bet on it.

· 4 ·

Today's Economies

The United States is entering a new era. The Republicans, by only a slim margin, control both the House and Senate, and the president is a Republican. We had this combination for only a short time in 2005–2006. Our new president is not a career politician and may be viewed as his own person with weaker party-line ties than we have seen in decades. In fact, records show he was a registered Republican before 2001, switched his registration to Democrat at that time, and then switched his party to Republican again in 2009. This new mix of powerful decision makers, and potentially less gridlock in Washington, will certainly have an impact on economic direction. But, as we've seen since 2009, there is only so much the government can do to impact the growth of our domestic economy.

MARKETS CRASH—IT'S A FACT OF LIFE

It would be difficult to shed any light on the current state of our economy without stepping back to 2008 to lay some groundwork.

The largest point drop of the Dow Jones Industrial Average occurred on September 29, 2008. Within the day, trading fell as much as 774.17 points. Reasons for the historic sell-off had been building for a while, but that day, most of the blame was placed on the decision by Congress to reject a bill that would have bailed out several troubled banks. Dow stocks had not been positive in 2008 after having reached a high on October 9, 2007, when they closed at 14,164.53 points. Less than 18 months later, Dow stocks had given up half their value, and on March 9, 2009, after an unrelenting fall, they traded at 6,547.05.

The period from December 2007 to June 2009 became known as the "Great Recession." The structure of our stock and bond markets has still not recovered from the various steps that were taken in response to the crisis. The first of these steps was taken in 2007 when the U.S. Federal Reserve Bank (the Fed) injected huge amounts of cash reserves into the banking system. The Fed did this to help banks that had been caught owning loans that were quickly going bad on properties declining in value. The Federal Reserve, which controls overnight lending rates between banks, dramatically lowered rates to an unheard of 0.25 percent. They told the markets that these rates would be held this low for an extended period in order to set market expectations and pull longer maturity interest rates down. A zero percent lending rate between banks helped stave off liquidity concerns and helped profitability for banks that had lent money long term at much higher rates.

This had limited positive impact, as bank troubles spread and mortgage defaults increased. With interest rates at or near zero percent, the Fed no longer had lowering interest rates as a tool to prop up the economy. They turned to an unproven policy tool they called *quantitative easing*. I view quantitative easing as a desperate policy tool—a last resort.

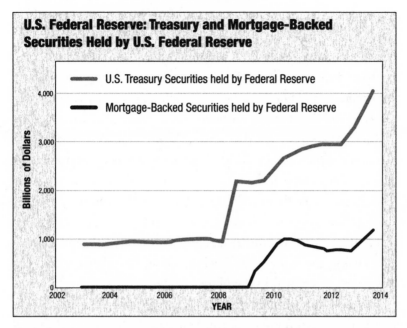

U.S. Federal Reserve: Treasury and Mortgage-Backed Securities Held by U.S. Federal Reserve

U.S. Treasury Securities held by Federal Reserve

Mortgage-Backed Securities held by Federal Reserve

Just One of the Ways the Federal Reserve Threw Money Into the Economy. Over a Seven Year Period the U.S. Treasury's Purchase of Securities to Shore-up Markets, Increased Fourfold.

'Modeled after https://commons.wikimedia.org/wiki/File:U.S._Federal_Reserve_-_Treasury_and_Mortgage-Backed_Securities_Held.png by Farcaster'

Quantitative easing, or QE, attempts to increase lending by banks, which stimulates growth. It also helps increase the supply of money in circulation and lowers interest rates across the board, even on riskier investments. The Federal Reserve carries this out by entering the bond market and purchasing a set dollar amount of bonds, including non-Treasuries, to lower interest rates and add money into the economy. From November 2008 to September 2012, three QE programs were implemented. The outcome for the Fed's balance sheet was that the securities they held ballooned from under $800 billion to over $4.0 trillion. In October 2014, the Federal Reserve indicated an end to the QE program. This was accomplished by halting trillions of dollars of bond purchases and allowing them to mature on schedule. These maturities are paid to the Fed, who was the owner. The net effect is that cash is taken out of the economy. Will the economy survive interest rates being raised to a more natural level and $4.0 trillion being taken out of the economy and bond markets? Unfortunately, there is no history for us to look back on for answers.* †

There's an expression that states, "When America sneezes, the rest of the world catches a cold." So, what happened internationally when America was in the hospital on life support? Without going into unnecessary detail, Europe, Asia, South America, and the Pacific Rim countries all experienced, and are still experiencing, difficult depressions and recessions. Many are struggling with them using the same tools, such as quantitative easing and low interest rates, applied in the United States.

I would not have subjected you to the numbers and inner workings of Fed policy if not to clearly demonstrate this point: The aftermath of the Great Recession will be with us for a long time. Reduced stimulus domestically and weak economies internationally suggest economic sluggishness will exist well past this decade.

SOME OTHER HEADWINDS

Here is some good news. According to statistics created by the Social Security Administration:

- "A man who reaches age 65 today can expect to live, on average, until age 84.3."

- "A woman who reaches age 65 today can expect to live, on average, until age 86.6."

---

* Source: http://www.federalreservehistory.org/Events/DetailView/58

† Source: http://voxeu.org/article/federal-reserve-policy-responses-crisis-2007-08

Even better news—"one out of every four of today's 65-year-olds will live past age 90."

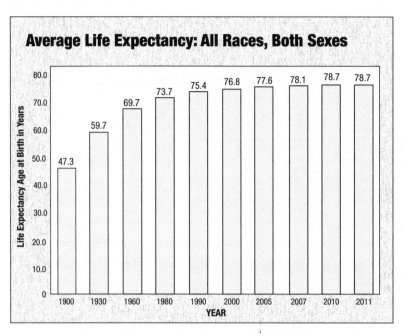

Average Life Expectancy: All Races, Both Sexes

Why, You Need to Plan for a Longer Retirement.
As life expectancy increases, retirees need to look for investments that provide income without touching the amount they have invested.

Source: http://www.infoplease.com/ipa/A0005148.html

This is good news, and in Chapter 5 on "Retirement Life" I will treat it as such and offer suggestions on how to make the most of this extra time. But this chapter is about today's economy, and the numbers on life expectancy presented are expected to be drags on the future economy.

The logic is simple: When people reach young adulthood, on average they are larger consumers. They are more likely to purchase a new home, furnish that home, buy cars more frequently, and upgrade much more than they are expected to 40 years later. They're also, on average, more productive. After all, they are in their working years and presumably providing goods and services that add to the country's gross domestic product (GDP). Later in life we are more likely to stay in the home we own, our needs for new appliances and other large or small purchases is not as high, and we don't consume as much as we used to. The unfortunate truth is, overall, that individuals living longer is a net negative on economic activity.

This being the case, our economy is in "double jeopardy." We're at a point in our history when we have a record number of people reaching retirement age. So, not only are retirees living longer, but there are more retirees than ever before, and that's growing. Mathematically, this results in a lower percent of young people, and young people are the spenders and producers. This all adds up, or in this case, subtracts out to economic weakness.

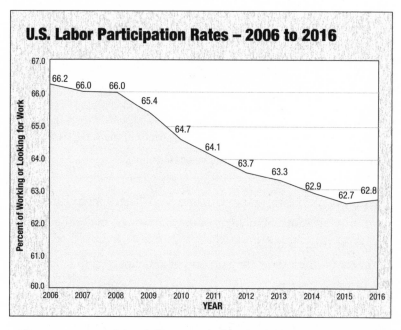

The percentage of the civilian population that is employed or unemployed that are actively searching for work. From 2006 through 2016 it's been the lowest participation rate in thirty or more years.

Source: https://data.bls.gov/timeseries/LNS11300000

THE NUMBERS

On average, every day, 10,000 Baby Boomers retire. I read this number a while back and at first I had a hard time believing it; since there are 365 days in a year, it seemed incredible to me that almost 4 million per year would retire. So, I checked it. I learned that not only does the Social Security Administration use a similar number, but a Pew Research report from December 2010 states, "On January 1, 2011, the oldest Baby Boomers will turn 65. Every day for the next 19 years, about 10,000 more will cross that threshold. By 2030, when all Baby Boomers will have turned 65, fully 18 percent of the nation's population will be at least that age." My final check to prove the validity of this huge number to myself, was to take out my calculator. There were 76 million Baby Boomers born from 1946 to 1964. That's a 19-year period, and 76 million divided by 19 years *is closer to 11,000 per day*.

At the same time that 4 million Americans will be leaving the workforce, there will be fewer entering. This is because two decades ago birthrates went down. As a gauge to this disparity, in 2017 there will only be 3.5 million high school graduates versus 4 million Baby Boomers entering retirement. That's 14 percent more taking themselves out of the workforce in just one year.[*]

If you're still not convinced that more people retiring (and living longer) is a negative for the economy, let me put on my CPA hat for a minute, and break it down to math:

GDP = Population Growth × Output per Person

If we use high school graduation as our growth rate, we know it is slowing. If we use retiring as a gauge of reduced output, we know

---

[*] Source: http://nces.ed.gov/fastfacts/display.asp?id=372

there is a reduction. Therefore, GDP won't rise and the economy, measured by GDP, will falter until one or both of these contributors to GDP changes.

THE NATIONAL DEBT

Debt has its place in our personal lives and, if used wisely, as a tool it can help a nation prosper or, in times of war, better defend itself. But when households use long-term debt to continually purchase items with short-term usefulness, they can get themselves in trouble. The loan has to be paid back, long after the payoff from the item has passed. The same is true for nations. If money is borrowed, especially at an increasing rate, to finance a lifestyle rather than investing in infrastructure and other expenditures with a long-term payoff, then paying off the loans with taxes has the effect of borrowing from future economic activity. In other words, money paid in taxes that will be used to pay off previous government folly will borrow from economic activity down the road.

Have we, as a nation, done this? I'll define the U.S. debt simply as the debt owed by the federal government to all lenders. As of late 2016 it is approaching $20 trillion. It's the largest in the world for a single country, close in size to all the debt of the 28 countries in the European Union. This is staggering. And it's unprecedented. With 325 million citizens it would take collecting over $61,000 from every man, woman and child to pay it off. That's much more than the average household earns in a year.

$$\$20,000,000,000,000 / 325,000,000 = \$61,538.46$$

This is how quickly the debt has grown over a 10-year period:

2006: $ 8.50 trillion
2007: $ 9.01 trillion
2008: $10.02 trillion
2009: $11.91 trillion
2010: $13.56 trillion
2011: $14.79 trillion
2012: $16.07 trillion
2013: $16.74 trillion
2014: $17.82 trillion
2015: $18.15 trillion
2016: $19.91 trillion

I mentioned that paying the debt back takes away from future activity. Keep in mind that interest rates are historically low; if they should begin to rise, the cost of paying this debt back will cost all of us even more.

Another concern that we should all be aware of is that as the debt matures, it is not reduced; instead, new securities are issued to pay off the holders. Rolling U.S. debt has not historically been a problem and has been easy recently, as demand for U.S. issued securities has been high. But the reason for this high demand is not necessarily a desire to invest in the United States. Instead, countries such as China are investing in U.S. Treasuries to hold U.S. dollars. The United States has the only reserve currency. That is the currency most accepted in any international transaction, including oil purchases. In recent years, with economic weakness globally, there has been demand for foreign countries, as well as foreign individuals, to own U.S. dollars (these dollars are typically stored in Treasury securities).

The U.S. dollar is used internationally much the way gold once was. And demand for it allows the dollar to maintain a high value globally and helps contribute to our high standard of living. But the U.S. dollar isn't gold. In fact, part of its strength lies in the world's oil transactions. Across the globe transactions with OPEC are in U.S. dollars. This relationship helps maintain strong demand for our currency, giving it resilience and buying power. This relationship could fall apart if faith in our ability to manage our finances drops below the faith of another country's economy.

Former head of PIMCO, Mohamed El-Erian, suggested in his book, aptly titled *The Only Game in Town*, that the dollar remains the world reserve currency only because we are the "best house in a bad neighborhood." This suggests that we don't have to be a particularly good house, just better than those that surround us. So, if other countries put their houses in better order, or if countries like China or India become more transparent and develop global trust, the United States may lose its status. This would put serious downward strain on both the economy and our purchasing power.

Can this happen? The countries I just mentioned are currently running budget surpluses, while the United States is running deficits. The main reason one of their currencies hasn't already reached world reserve status are the issues of transparency in their monetary policies; their accounting rules are not aligned with much of the world and, most importantly, their economies are not as open to trade.

THE TIPPING POINT

Does the United States have a problem? A country's debt-to-GDP ratio is the ratio of its national debt to its gross domestic product. By comparing what a country owes to what it produces, the debt-to-GDP ratio indicates the ability to pay back what the country borrowed. Often expressed as a percentage, the ratio can be interpreted as the number of years needed to pay back debt if GDP is dedicated entirely to debt repayment.

Here's a good way to look at it. The U.S. debt-to-GDP ratio has been escalating at a pace sure to cause concern among outsiders holding U.S. dollars. In the mid-1970s through the early 1980s, our debt-to-GDP ratio stood solidly at 30 to 31 percent. Then borrowing began to escalate faster than growth. By 1995, the amount of debt-to-GDP was over 65 percent; that's more than twice as high as it was 15 years earlier. Today it stands at 105 percent.

Where is the tipping point that puts a nation at risk of facing a crisis? We are not currently in a crisis, but by anyone's measure of the high debt-to-GDP in the United States and from what much of my studies reveal, anything over 80 percent is cause for concern.*

POTENTIAL BRIGHT SPOT

Most of the points I've made in this chapter about the current state of the economy reflect information I use in discussions in my TV appearances, public speaking engagements, and in discussions with clients or other advisors who ask my thoughts. I have never laid it out all at once, though, and it seems more frightening than I had hoped. After all, there's no denying the economy is fragile—stocks are expensive based on P/E ratios, stock market history suggests a sustained stock sell-off could be imminent, interest rates are likely to rise, stimulus provided by QE is left to run-off, there is no economic strength internationally to lift the United States, aging Baby Boomers are expected to spend less in retirement while living longer in retirement and the high national debt will borrow from growth. The U.S. debt-to-GDP ratio adds to these risk factors.

---

* Source: https://www.washingtonpost.com/news/wonk/wp/2013/02/22/
is-there-a-tipping-point-for-government-debt-and-is-the-united-states-
about-to-hit-it/?utm_term=.8c7f27a70c48

This all suggests that investing in securities that rely on a strong economy is not a safe bet. It probably goes even further to suggest that it's an improbable bet where the investor risks a great deal for very little gain.

Despite the issues that I just laid out, believe it or not I am a very optimistic person. I'm also a realist. The leadership in Washington has dramatically changed. The House, the Senate, and the executive branch will now all be the same party. There can be no more finger-pointing or any voting against or for a bill because that is what the party prefers. The Republican party and the Democrats are left having to redefine themselves after the election. Let's hope they do it with the country's best interest at heart.

Whether you're a fan of President Donald Trump or not, there's no denying he's a natural politician; in this campaign, he clearly "out-politicked" his opponents. There isn't enough data to surmise that Trump has the potential to keep the next market crash at bay. But as a businessman, he may have a better chance than others. I've always felt that, economically, the country should be run like a business. And if he moves us closer to that model, it could end up being a good thing for the markets and economic growth at least for a while.

It can't be all that bad to put *America first* when making decisions. He'll make mistakes, no doubt, but overall I believe he's good for business, and business is what makes America Great.

· 5 ·

Retirement Life

Do you have a clear vision of what your retirement will look like?
If you're not yet retired, you may be in the position that many of
my clients find themselves. They're looking forward to not having
to go to work, yet it's awkward for them wishing themselves older.
For my long-term clients, I've found retirement means increased
options and, conversely, decreased options. What I counsel people
to do is plan now to reduce the side that decreases options. Take
care of your health to the extent you can, as well as your finances
as early in life as possible. This will allow more options for what
you can do with your time, and you will give up less if your financial means are both higher and more certain.

After years of meeting with many people, what I have discovered is that they do a decent job of saving money but they haven't
taken time to think about goals for retirement. As a result, they
haven't thought about the appropriate strategy to support their
goals. Consequently, I have found that many times their current
financial strategy is in direct conflict with their goals. This can be
catastrophic!

Setting realistic goals is important, and couples should begin discussing their individual expectations with each other long before they work their last day. I have seen cases where couples tell me they want to travel the world, or buy a house for their son or daughter, yet the income and savings they have to work with won't allow it.

What I have found from my conversations with other advisors around the country, articles I've read, and even my own clients is that retirement does not often lead to whirlwind travels or other major life changes. More often people tend to focus a bit more on hobbies and activities closer to home that change their quality of life in retirement without adding huge expense.

I like to hold discussions with clients while they are still working and calculate for them the expenses they won't have or that will be reduced in retirement. Many don't consider how much they will be reducing costs after work. Often there is an incredible sigh of relief when they realize that retirement, which will almost always reduce their income, also will reduce many of their expenses.

Think about clothing, convenience food, and transportation costs that escalate when you're working. The truth is, most retirees spend less, sometimes much less, than they did while working.

In 2014, the Bureau of Labor Statistics (BLS)[*] reported that in the period just before retirement, defined as between ages 55 to 64, workers had average expenditures of $56,267. The study also looked at retirees between the ages of 65 to 74 and found their annual outlays were $48,885—or $7,382 less!

---

[*] Source: https://www.bls.gov/opub/btn/volume-5/spending-patterns-of-older-americans.htm

NET CHANGES TO COSTS IN RETIREMENT

Housing is an expense not easily avoided. The BLS survey found that these costs decline from an average of $18,006 for the group aged 55 to 64, to $15,838 for those between 65 to 74 years of age. How is this possible? Retirees may pay off the mortgage or downsize as they get older.

Food cost is a reduction that most don't consider. You're not going to eat less in retirement, but there is less of a need to spend on more expensive, time-saving options such as eating in restaurants or other, more pricy ready-to-eat options. The luxury for many retirees becomes being able to prepare their own food with the extra time they have. How much is saved? According the BLS government report, those just before retirement had average annual food expenditures of $6,800, while those post-retirement spent $6,303.

How much is your commute to work costing you? This is the most significant way retirees save money. The cost of transportation declines incrementally with age. For those in the age range of 55 to 64, the BLS calculated the cost to average $9,321. For retirees between the ages of 65 to 74, the cost dropped to $8,338. And as people advanced past their 75th birthday, the cost of transportation averaged just $5,091 per year.

Retirees experience a reduced need for expensive consumer goods, including higher-priced work clothing. Household appliances are replaced less often, and furniture is also replaced less frequently.

When I sit down with clients to discuss how their expenses will change in retirement, there is one budget item they hadn't given much thought to. Yet it's the most obvious, and usually a large part of their annual budget. When people leave their employment to retire, they no longer put away money for retirement. They don't contribute to a 401(k) or an individual retirement account (IRA), and they no longer pay into Social Security. According to the study cited, these contributions drop from an average of $6,578 for workers nearing retirement to just $2,788 among those ages 65 to 74. I believe you can calculate your own exact numbers very easily.

I wanted to end Section 1 with this abbreviated chapter on retirement life for two reasons. First, people head into retirement with unrealistic expectations of how they will actually use the additional time they have, so I provided a list of popular options for you to see where you might actually use your increased time. Second, I want to make sure you understand that a lack of options due to income reduction may not exist in your situation. Retirement usually requires less income than people initially think.

SECTION 2
LAYING THE GROUNDWORK

· 6 ·

Vetting Financial Advisors to Find the Right Match

Deep in the first chapter I promised Section 2 would provide information and guidance for you to find the right investments without being encumbered by currently accepted ideas that no longer hold true. Well, you made it through Section 1 and deserve a break from statistics, economics, and history. This section lays the groundwork for developing common sense income strategies. Whether you're a do-it-yourselfer who is considering going it alone, someone deciding to work with a financial advisor, or someone who has had a relationship with an advisor for many years, it's important to understand how to be comfortable that your decision is best for you. And it's just as important to make sure your current advisor is equipped and is best suited to implement a financial plan that truly supports your retirement goals.

DO YOU EVEN NEED A FINANCIAL ADVISOR?

You've brought your family through many challenges, and perhaps managed a business or a department at work. You can add, subtract, and read the financial papers. Why would you want to bring someone else into the picture who will ask a lot of personal questions about health and money and go through your financial information? Perhaps you don't. Many people enjoy managing their own investment portfolio. If you don't enjoy keeping up with new alternatives, required minimum distributions, tax planning, new regulations, and hundreds of choices to make over the course of your retirement, you may stand to save thousands by hiring a competent financial advisor who specializes in the strategies we will discuss in this book.

Managing your own money successfully can be very fulfilling, but considering the decisions and their possible outcomes, it can be very risky. Here are the three attributes I believe are required of a do-it-yourselfer:

How well do you OBJECTIVELY CONSIDER information?

There is a great deal of hype and even misinformation floating around investment websites, financial TV programs, and publications. It's important to be able to discern the information from the buzz surrounding it. This is often as easy as following the money. In Section 1 of the book, I gave many examples of who benefits from you investing a certain way. It's important that you can read the signs and analyze alternatives and the probabilities of their success without being clouded by emotions. Make sure you have a reliable way to correctly track your investment performance. Investors often suffer from only counting their best investments, while ignoring the poor performers. Many times those poor investments would be better off sold and replaced with a higher performing asset.

What is your PURPOSE?

This seems simple enough, but it's so important I have dedicated all of Chapter 11 to helping readers get this right. Most people who come through my door looking to fire their current financial advisor and hire someone else are there because they weren't invested in a strategy that supported their purpose. They were placed in a one-size-fits-all portfolio or, worse, were at the whim of someone who felt certain they had a crystal ball to pick stocks. Most never realized they weren't invested properly to reach their goals until their investments went way off track.

How much of your TIME can you devote to your money?

Staying current on stocks, bonds, currencies, ETFs, and REITs doesn't have to be a full-time job, but if you honestly can't devote at least a couple of hours a week to monitoring your portfolio against the various markets, you may not be the right person for the job.

It's important to note that if you did not intend to be a do-it-yourselfer and are in retirement with a 401(k) that you have not rolled into an IRA, you have in effect decided that you are managing your money. There is a very good chance that you are already losing or wasting money and could benefit from a good advisor. (More on this in Chapter 14).

Keep in mind that tending to your own investments does not have to be an all-or-nothing decision. Almost everyone will have reason to outsource some of their financial planning. Sometimes they bring in an expert in annuities, or an estate planner, or tax professional. You may find it best to let someone better suited to parts of the process take the lead on a few items.

QUESTIONS TO ASK FINANCIAL ADVISORS

Maybe you've decided that a good financial advisor will provide a better level of attention and comprehend the financial landscape better than you. It's a lot of responsibility to place in the hands of someone—after all, your future is literally at stake.

There are a variety of different advisors who specialize differently. Although there is overlap in the services they provide, they don't all do the same thing. The majority of the clients that retain my services are looking for a trusted financial advisor who understands the income needs of today's retiree. Here are a few questions to help you in your quest to find the right advisor for your situation:

1. Are you bound to a fiduciary standard?

There are two standards that advisors are held to when offering financial advice. They are the "suitability" standard and the "fiduciary" standard. The suitability standard is the weakest of the two. It only requires that the investments fit the client's risk tolerance and overall objectives. The advisor does not have to suggest investments that are likely to provide an even better fit or lower client cost. In fact, there are many cases of advisors of low integrity recommending the least suitable option within the spectrum of suitability. Unfortunately, unsuspecting clients may be missing out on the alternative if their advisors looks to maximize income to themselves by selling something they make more money on, rather than maximizing return and lowering risk to the client.

If your advisor is only held to the suitability standard, you may wish to look for one held to a fiduciary standard.

The fiduciary standard requires advisors to act in the best interest of the person they are providing advice for, period. There is no wiggle room. I believe that most advisors are trustworthy and honest, but compensation in the business is set up to invite some level of conflict and temptation. The fiduciary standard is a regulatory way to remove the temptation for most.

If the advisor is acting under the fiduciary standard and tells you so, don't be afraid to get it in writing.

2. How are you compensated?

This is important to understand because for every dollar made from your account is a dollar that is not working to earn you income. Like any other service you consume, the provider must offer enough value for the service to be worth your while.

The most popular form of compensation for a financial advisor is commission and fees. These advisors are often affiliated with a large financial services company such as Morgan Stanley, Merrill Lynch, and others. Their compensation comes from fees on assets under management and products sold, such as annuities.

Some advisors are not beholden to the products of any specific large financial company. They typically are self-employed and not obligated to any specific family of products or offerings. They can literally pick and choose from a wider array of options while fulfilling their clients' objectives. This is a big plus when you are shopping for an advisor.

Whether your advisor is fee-based or is compensated through commission and fees, you will want to know what the fees are. Although cheaper does not always mean better, if the advisor fees are above the range of 1.0 to 1.5 percent, you should question what you're getting for your money.

3. What is your experience with situations like mine?

There are excellent advisors who focus on college planning that you wouldn't want to hire for retirement planning (even if they are your nephew). And there are excellent retirement planners who don't have enough experience to do justice to a large family trust. Among the advisor universe, find an advisor that is experienced in your situation.

As an added measure, ask about their designations and registrations. I am a CPA (certified public accountant), which is arguably among the highest financial designations, requiring the most schooling, continuing education, and testing. I am also a personal financial specialist (PFS), which is a financial planning designation only available to CPAs.

Other popular designations and registrations you'll see are CFP (certified financial planner), CFS (certified fund specialist), ChFC (chartered financial consultant), CFA (chartered financial analyst), CLU (chartered life underwriter), FINRA registrations Series 7, 24, 51, 63, 65, 66, and insurance licenses.

4. What is your philosophy regarding managing client accounts?

This is a good overall question to determine if you're the right fit with the advisor. If they answer in ways that suggest they may be too risky or too risk-averse for your appetite, they may not be a good fit for you. If they answer in a manner that suggests they have not been paying attention to your goals and what the purpose of the account is, then they clearly aren't a good fit. Does the advisor sound like a salesman who sells investment ideas and products, or an investment person who sells as part of their business? Stay away from anyone who appears to be a salesman first. That won't help you develop and implement a strategy to support your goals.

5. Who is their ideal client?

This is related to the previous question, but it digs deeper to help you decide if the person sitting in front of you understands your situation and has the skills and knowledge to accomplish what you need. A red flag would be if the advisor appears to take on as a client anyone who walks through the door.

6. What's the stock market going to do?

This question is a little sneaky, but you want to make sure the advisor doesn't believe they have the ability to do what very high-paid "experts" fail at every day. That is, calling the stock market. They should have an overall opinion, but that opinion should not stand in the way of them providing assets to invest in that are not speculative, but instead provide the right balance of reward and risk. Often retirement accounts should not tolerate much risk.

WHAT NOT TO SAY TO A FINANCIAL ADVISOR

1. Just do what you want.

It's very important to place a great deal of confidence in the person or team you choose to manage your assets. But it is you who are ultimately responsible and it is your household that has to live with the results. Ronald Reagan used to say: "Trust, but verify."* Take an active role in understanding how you are invested and why.

The fact that you're reading this book is already a good start in gaining important knowledge. Make sure that you meet with your advisor at a minimum of once a year to discuss any changes in your situation, and for any reason that your assets have not or may not accomplish what they were set out to do. Use this book to discover useful terminology to improve your understanding. Keep an ear open and an eye out for when determinations are being

---

* Source: by Suzanne Massie http://trustbutverifybook.com/ and Source: https://en.wikipedia.org/wiki/Trust,_but_verify
https://www.leadergrow.com/articles/443-trust-but-verify

made, to make sure the risk levels of your holdings are comfortable for you.

If the advisor sees that you are taking an active role, they are more likely to explain your options and be more attentive to your account. View your communication with your financial advisor as you would meeting with a doctor or other respected professional: The more knowledge and communication you have with your advisor, the higher your probability of getting exactly what you want.

2. What's your performance?

I understand why this question is asked constantly, but the answer, if stated in terms of a percent return, may be useless. The answer would have to be that clients have different needs and therefore different performance. How closely matched any performance is to the client's plan and goals is the true measure of success. And of course, any advisor would be negligent if they didn't state up-front that past performance is not an indication of future results.

Answering this question may also lead the potential client down the wrong path. Because a large percent of my clients are in or near retirement, they have very low risk portfolios. My clients view the success of their investment strategy in comparison to their goals. Personally, I know how high my risk-adjusted return has been to them, even if they are only moderately aware.

3. Will I be invited on your annual dinner cruise for clients?

Although people aren't usually as direct as this, I have found many choosing an advisor because of other perks. Trust me, this is not how you want to choose your advisor. Look instead at how well your advisor can safely put your money to work and you can treat yourself with the additional income.

4. You manage my neighbor's accounts. How are they invested?

All financial advisors are bound by confidentiality rules that prevent them from even recognizing that your neighbors are their client unless they have the neighbor's permission. This may seem like a friendly discussion item, but understand the advisor cannot answer you.

NO ONE CAN PREDICT THE FUTURE

When vetting financial advisors, it's important to realize that the investment advice should not rely on predicting the future. If it's income you will need in retirement, thinking someone can pick stocks or predict the stock market can be fatal to a sound retirement strategy.

Great advisors understand their role is staying up to date on all that may benefit you and your objectives. What's essential is a solid plan that's used as a roadmap and then adhered to until either your situation changes or better options become available. Financial planning is, in the final analysis, about being equipped with all the potential ingredients and then finding the right combination to bake into your plan.

If you are vetting yourself to see if you should manage your own assets, remember the do-it-yourself approach requires intense discipline. I have met people with all the knowledge they need but who went astray by listening to a friend or a TV personality who told them "you can't go wrong." Individuals are more likely to deviate from a good plan than a well-vetted advisor.

· 7 ·

How I Got to Where I Am

"You don't buy drumsticks from a piano teacher."

—*Michael Eastham*

A few months back my son was headed to a music store to get guitar strings and I suggested he speak with someone who works there who plays guitar. I didn't think too much about it when I said it, but it only makes sense to get a recommendation from someone with the most expertise in the particular instrument than from someone who is an expert is brass or percussion instruments.

The advice makes just as much sense for those seeking financial advice. Seek out the expert who has the most experience, demonstrates solid knowledge, and specializes in what you need. Then make certain the advisor listens, understands, and most important cares.

This is what clients tell me separates my practice at Fellowship Financial Group from all the others. They tell me that it's clear I care deeply about the outcome for them of their plan. I often see additional solutions that may benefit their situation. I'm happy they see this because as successful as my practice is, it's all worthwhile because of the people I'm helping. Too many people are in this business and want their investors to think they have a crystal ball or have exceptionally clear insight about what tomorrow will bring. I never make that promise. What I promise is that if you are investing for retirement, I will work with you to determine what you need and first work to reduce investment risk, then find the most sound means to make sure you arrive safely at your destination.

My business continues to grow rapidly simply because if you do the right thing it comes back to you in multiples. I see evidence of this every month. I've had more than one new client come out of one of the classes that I give and do nothing for three or four years. Then seemingly out of the blue they schedule a meeting to come in and see me. Often they had some sort of triggering event and remember something I said which they kept in the back of their mind. My advisory practice is probably not unique in this way, but I find I have fans out there I never knew about. Some of my referrals come from people who didn't do business with me.

One funny story occurred a couple of years ago when a gentleman came in for tax services and said all of his retirement assets were tied up in annuities. Someone not purpose-based may have suggested taking the money out of the annuities and rolling them into some whiz-bang new product to help him get more. This man even asked me if there was something new under the sun that would be more beneficial. I told him that he was fine. I may have been able to match what he owned, but I knew I couldn't exceed it. I instead explained to him exactly what he owned. A few months later he sent in a good friend of his who needed tax work and an investment plan, and a month after that, he referred two more. Greed destroys many advisors in this business; I find that the more giving of sound advice I am, the better everyone, including me, does.

PEOPLE IN OR NEAR RETIREMENT NEED SOUND ADVICE

We're living at a time when those approaching or even in retire-ment, the so-called Income Generation, need to better understand realities. If people's memories about investing ended in the 1970s or even 1987, when the stock market crashed, they may not be as inclined to take risk—risk that may serve them well, but could also permanently destroy any chance they have of retiring.

Following 1987 we had a boom period, and the 1990s created a false sense of comfort with the stock market. It has never been secure. During the 1990s, investors became used to 12 – 15 percent returns and have been looking for a repeat of those returns ever since. This creates an unrealistic expectation that can lead to risk-ing their entire portfolio for an additional 2 percent return, as we have experienced since the beginning of the 21st century. In addi-tion to the expectations set during the end of the last millennia, the media has propagated expectations of 10 to 12 percent returns in stocks. Is it possible? Yes, stocks go up and stocks go down, so depending on your entrance and exit it is probably available every single year. Of course, trying to achieve this may also destroy 10 to 50 percent of your wealth. Does that make sense for retirees who would have to go back to work if they eroded 20 percent or more of their retirement savings? Certainly not. I caution anyone not to put their retirement future in the hands of an advisor pretending they will deliver double-digit returns.

It's difficult, because for every fear-driven person there are three greed-driven individuals. This is especially hard when stocks are having a great year. It moves up, more people get in, it moves up more, then there's peer pressure to do what your neighbors are doing, so it continues up and your clients begin to wonder why they aren't experiencing the growth their neighbors are. Then BOOM, the market drops. That's when my phone rings and people want to come in for safer alternatives.

I am honest to a fault with my clients and one of the things I tell them when they sit down with me is, "If you invest with me, if you allow me the privilege of being your financial planner, then you're probably not going to have bragging rights at cocktail parties. What you're likely to see is predictable income and a reasonable expectation of returns. And you're likely to sleep better at night."

The clients most eager to benefit from my firm's area of expertise are those who realize that it is better to arrive at your destination than to race and risk crashing along the way or not making your destination at all. Planning is key here.

A well-designed income strategy should instill confidence that you will accomplish your financial goals on time. If your investments appear to be doing great one year but lousy the next, that's called speculating. Imagine you were sitting in an airplane at the gate. The pilot announces, "Folks I'm pretty sure we have enough fuel to make our destination. I'll do my best." What would you do? It's interesting how we would never take that risk with our physical lives but somehow it's acceptable when it comes to our financial lives. No one can plan that way, and no one wants to *have* to go back to work after they retire.

TWO THINGS I WISH EVERYONE UNDERSTOOD
(The problem with having a different tune)

Number one—Most financial planners, investment advisors, and stock brokers tout their performance. They teach us to look at performance. Even Morningstar, which is supposed to be an investor resource, bases its reporting on performance. Performance can be misleading. So, as I said earlier, there will always be someone in

Michael on Fox Business Network's Varney and Co. February 11th, 2016

Michael on CNBC during the Market Sell Off August 24th, 2015

your circle of friends or at a cocktail party bragging about their performance.

Retirement assets should be invested for your purpose. I go into detail in Chapter 11 about how performance measurements set retirees up for disappointment and even hardship. I like to bring up this idea often and early, because it is a huge paradigm shift that will take time for most readers. By trying to achieve performance goals, people tend to take on more risk than they might be aware of. A purpose-based investor is someone who asks the question. *"How much income do I need?"*

In many cases investors don't need the 12 percent they yearn for and take on too much risk. A few years ago, a widow came into my office after losing 40 percent in her investments. I asked her what happened. She said her advisor told her she should be earning 10-12 percent in the market. So that's the way he invested. By the time she was so sick to her stomach that she had to pull her investments, she had lost 40 percent. I said, "Did your advisor ever ask you how much income you need in order to live for the rest of your life?" She looked at me as if I had three heads. So we did the math, and discovered she only needed 4 percent income from her investments to keep her comfortable for the rest of her life. Consider the difference in risk level between investing for 4 percent rather than 12 percent. That's the difference between performance and purpose-based investing.

I run the numbers for different people in different scenarios every week, and what they need to live comfortably in retirement is many times less than half of that 12 percent. They can achieve that without the risk of raising their blood pressure. They don't teach this in financial planning school, and I don't see it mentioned in magazine articles or popular retirement planning websites, yet my clients are living proof that earning a more predictable income and knowing what to expect is what we should be hearing in the media and in schools. When I make my TV appearances, I bring it up when I get a chance.

WHY I SPECIALIZE IN INCOME STRATEGIES AND RETIREMENT

Before becoming a financial advisor I was a CPA in the corporate finance world. One of my areas of expertise was exit strategies. Although exiting from the workforce is a bit different, I have a more significant background than most advisors who are not CPAs. It's been very helpful in offering real value. I advise people who come to my classes in no uncertain terms what should be on their front burner.

These include implementing and reviewing their strategies for required minimum distributions, social security, taxes, and estate planning, as well as developing an understanding of income-generating investments. People are so grateful for the help and my background—not just in terms of education. Recent TV appearances on Fox Business News also certainly gives the audience confidence.

PATRIOTISM IS IMPORTANT TO ME

My business and home are both in Florida. The primary reason for moving to the Sunshine State from Maryland was, well, sunshine. It has become home for me and my family. I've come to take for granted the all-year-round warmth and, as a businessman, a zero income tax rate.

Those who know me also know how much I love being an American. So much of what we have in this country we take for granted and shouldn't. When I start to forget, one of my clients who immigrated here from overseas is sure to remind me. First and foremost, we have unsurpassed freedom. We have government stability and military strength, and if you want to build something from scratch, there is no one to stop you. I'm living proof of that. I started out wanting to become a drummer. Then I went to school, built a thriving business, and I'm now frequently on top financial TV programs, host my own radio show (Retirement Income Doctor) and if you're reading this, it means I've become a successful author, too. I'm grateful for the opportunity this country has provided (not handed) to me, and allowed me to achieve with hard work.

We've had our setbacks, but I'm certain the United States will always find its way back to being well-centered. Our Founding Fathers built the country on timeless principles that rely on Truth with a capital "T." Time shouldn't change some things. One of these is the ability to be a self-made person, which for obvious reasons is a very dear privilege to me. It's also one of the foundational reasons that our nation has achieved such a high level of economic greatness.

Our children shouldn't be taught that they are entitled to much more than opportunity. In fact, our Founding Fathers stated it clearly in the Declaration of Independence: *Life, liberty and the pursuit of happiness.* Our leaders and schools should demonstrate the importance of integrity, that you should be the same person on and off the field. Your character shouldn't be worn like a tie and come off when no one can see you. I believe very strongly in this, and I am certain it is this level of always pursuing the right thing that has taken me this far and helps to keep my clients happy.

· 8 ·

The Seven Pillars of Wealth

Life doesn't just give you things—you have to earn them. I learned this as a young adult the hard way, but I never stop teaching and preaching. In my business the obvious carryover is in developing a workable plan that carries clients in and through retirement. The plans aren't magic, and at times aren't easy, but without a plan, without earning in retirement, it is very difficult to successfully achieve it.

There are many books and articles that discuss the key ingredients, or the pillars that work together and hold up family finances. This is my own list, which I have developed from having seen hundreds of financial situations, both successful and unsuccessful. The concepts are fairly basic, but I'd be remiss if I didn't include them in this section because one doesn't have to be born into financial privilege or have been blessed with a very high paying job to achieve financial freedom. Many 9 to 5 people become the proverbial "millionaire next door."

FIRST PILLAR—FAMILY

Almost all of our early values come from family. For most of us, we didn't inherit the family farm or business. As we moved from an agricultural society to manufacturing and now a service-oriented economy, we are all left to our own devices to determine a career on our own. The family farm or family business is less of an option for most of us. But this doesn't mean that family doesn't play a big part in wealth. We still have values that have been handed down to us and that we can pass down ourselves.

In fact, according to a poll by the U.S. Trust*, the family plays a significant role in determining financial success. They asked people what they thought were the three most important values stressed in their families while they were growing up. The top three responses included academic achievement, financial discipline, and participation in the workplace. As a financial advisor, CPA, and a father of four, I was not surprised to read that among the financially successful, eight out of ten said their parents were firm disciplinarians but encouraged them to pursue their own interests and talents. Three-quarters of those answering said they had parents who were active in their lives both physically and emotionally.

This is even more critical than ever, as corporate employers have become less parental than ever before. For example, in 1983 there were 175,000 pension plans offered by employers; today there are less than 25,000. Many of these are no longer offered to new employees. Companies are also more inclined to let go of workers than they were in the past. All of this requires a first pillar of self-reliance which, at least in my experience, is best started at home when people are young.

---

* Source: http://www.forbes.com/sites/maggiemcgrath/2016/05/23/the-6-most-important-wealth-building-lessons-from-multi-millionaires/#6172139e6620

SECOND PILLAR—COMMON SENSE

Remain vigilant and don't become the victim of a high-pressure sales pitch that promises improbably high rewards. The expression, "If it sounds too good to be true it probably is," cannot be stated strongly enough. I've spoken to many very bright people who have come through my office door who made only one bad decision, and their finances are forever changed for the worse.

Bernie Madoff's Ponzi scheme, which began to unravel in 2009, is the perfect example. Although the returns that Madoff paid were considered by many to be mathematically impossible, investors—including many very successful businesspeople—poured money into his fraud. Madoff stole headlines that year from others such as Scott Rothstein and Arthur Nadel, whose large Ponzi schemes also defrauded thousands of otherwise bright people of billions of dollars.

You don't want to miss out on true opportunity. Here are some questions you can ask before handing over a single dollar.

- Is the salesperson pressuring me to make an immediate decision? It's best to walk away if you don't have time to do any due diligence on an investment.

- Is the investment regulated? Common regulatory bodies are the Securities and Exchange Commission (SEC), state insurance departments, various stock exchanges, and the Federal Deposit Insurance Corporation (FDIC). Regulatory oversight is no guarantee of a good investment, but it helps if the investment comes under the umbrella of a large regulatory entity.

- When will the benefit from the investment be paid? Is it guaranteed, and by whom?

- How can I use a third party (not the seller) to monitor any change in value of the investment?

We live in a world where not everyone is comfortable making an honest living. Some of the schemes that damage the finances of smart people have been perpetrated by heartless individuals, and some are people who started out with a small lie that slowly grew. It doesn't matter. The effect on your account is the same.

I'll repeat: Use common sense, and if it sounds too good to be true, it probably is.

THIRD PILLAR—DILIGENCE

Choosing the right financial path requires diligence—diligence in selection of the path, and diligence and perseverance to stay on a chosen path. There will always be people trying to make us question our judgment. They will come in the form of TV analysts touting investments you've already deemed too risky. They will come in the form of financial salespeople trying to sway your direction to better feather their nest. Sometimes temptation will come in the form of purchases you'd like to make such as a new car, but doing so would sidetrack the much more important goal of being ready for retirement when you arrive.

FOURTH PILLAR—BE FORWARD-LOOKING

Never forget that the future is going to arrive whether you're ready for it or not. Preparing for the future is by far the best way to meet it when it arrives. Looking forward at what you want to accomplish financially and setting priorities is critical for success. If you're over the age of 45, this is how your priorities probably should be ranked.

Retirement: As self-serving as this may seem, considering that I manage money for retirees, I assure you it is extremely important. Social Security will not be enough for you to exist on, and each year your life expectancy has been increasing. Inflation has been tame in recent years, but history suggests it may not remain that way. Plan for the worst by putting away what you can now.

Build your rainy-day fund: Families without adequate backup cash are at times decimated by surprise expenses, which could include medical, home repair, job loss, or divorce.

Pay down debt: I intentionally placed debt third in order of importance, that doesn't mean it is unimportant. Managing your debt level is a great way to save interest charges and free up money for use in an emergency or to invest. It comes well ahead of expenses that are luxuries. The order that makes the most sense to pay down debt is to begin with credit cards, then generally work off other debt in order of highest interest rate first.

FIFTH PILLAR—INVEST

"Pay yourself first" is one of the pillars that is always included in lists like this. The best way to do this is by setting yourself up with an automatic deduction that goes to a savings or investment account. These preauthorized deposits will force you to find ways to live on less or not make frivolous purchases. Consistent saving or investing is less painful than lump-sum investing and keeps your financial health going in a positive direction. If you're not yet doing this, I suggest you start today.

SIXTH PILLAR—PLAIN VANILLA

We've all heard stories of investors who piled a bunch of money into the stock of a start-up or some other fast-moving company and the stockholder did well. This is not how most investors make their money for retirement, and it isn't a good strategy to ensure success.

The plain vanilla approach to investing includes strategies as well as the types of investments. In order to make sure you get to your destination you should not try to exceed a safe speed. By this I mean, don't look for high-flying stocks or promises of dubiously high returns. Instead, save regularly and create a portfolio of investment-grade securities and other sound companies that have been around a long time. Find shares that have paid regular dividends over an extended period and set it so the dividends reinvest. This is called a *dividend reinvestment plan*, or DRIP account, and it is a very good way to experience increased assets, without trying to find the next Apple or Amazon.

SEVENTH PILLAR—PAY ATTENTION TO TAXES

The compounding effect of investing makes it imperative that you become a tax-efficient investor in order to retain and earn maximum return on assets.

What you should look to do is measure how much you earned after you've paid the IRS. This, after all, is your actual return.

Outside of retirement accounts such as 401(k)s, IRAs, and 403(b)s, investments that pay regular interest or dividends are generally less appealing than those that rely on growth. This is because investments held outside of these accounts are generally taxed in the year received and not deferred.

Within qualified retirement accounts you should make sure you're saving as much as you can for retirement pretax before saving after taxes. The compounding effect of money pays big dividends over time. The same holds true for withdrawals. Pay attention to those withdrawals that have the most severe tax costs first.

WHY YOU SHOULD REVISIT THIS CHAPTER

Whether you're playing an instrument, participating in a sport, or practicing a safer investment strategy, it's smart to check your form now and then. Make sure you are doing the small things consistently that will make you a better musician, a more effective athlete, or a wealthier investor. Check back to this section on the Seven Pillars so that you can readjust anywhere you may be slipping.

· 9 ·

Know Thyself

When my wife and I first moved to Florida, she and another mom were homeschooling our kids. They decided they would also start an enrichment program where the kids would get more interaction and play with others. This led them to create a small soccer program. It turned out there was a good deal of need for this kind of program. In a very short time, we had 65 kids playing a bunch of different teams. Other parents quickly volunteered to coach and help in other ways, and 65 kids grew over 12 years to 230 kids, from age 3 on up, all benefiting from the program.

One of the unexpected benefits I've always gotten is watching kids and how they interact competitively. God makes us all different. The three-year-olds from a distance are playing what I call swarm soccer, and if you don't know them you may think they are all the same. When you get up close, you realize they are miniature versions of their future selves: Some are braggarts, others are naturally talented, some are very insecure, others are very afraid of getting hurt, and there are even some who would rather be home playing video games. The main reason the kids are brought to the field is first and foremost to have fun. As a coach/adult/parent, I can tell you they are gaining equally important, albeit less obvious, life skills. Among them: strategy, working together with a team, keep going even when you're tired, never take your eye off the ball, don't forget your goal, others will cheat, strive for constant improvement, and not everything is for everybody. There are hundreds of other nuanced learning opportunities, but one lesson I have seen time and again among the older kids is that all the skills in the world are useless unless you can put them to work. You may be able to run, kick, pass, block shots, and score in practice, but if you don't have a solid inner game on the field that holds you together and puts those skills to work, you will fall behind less outwardly skilled players. The coaches with winning teams among teenagers taught them to work on their inner game as well as the skills they need in the game.

This idea exists off the field as well. I have met many people who have great ideas for how to manage their own finances, but can't implement them. This is rarely spoken about in investment books such as this one, because it's either unknown by the author or considered an immeasurable that the author was afraid to write about.

HOW TO BE A MORE SUCCESSFUL INVESTOR

Do you want more financial and investment success? Look inside. "Know thyself"—be honest about your emotions when it comes to spending, borrowing, saving, and as we'll cover now, investing. Most of us are sophisticated enough to know that we should avoid emotion and use data and reason when making investments and other money decisions. I'm willing to bet that for every 100 investors who think they're relying completely on analytics and probabilities, there are 99 where emotions are working under the surface in ways they don't recognize. Those 99 don't know themselves as well as they think.

There are as many reasons for this to be true for the 50-year-old planning for retirement as there are for the 15-year-old preparing to take a shot in a soccer game. As Humans, we don't want to lose, and this often undermines the best and clearest course of action. At every age we have a strong propensity to regret the times when things didn't work out perfectly, and we often avoid action rather than implement a sound strategy that may not turn out perfectly. If we better understand how we feel, how we think, and what kind of personality we have, we get more insight into the forces that affect our investing behavior. That might make us smarter investors—or at least make us invest in ways that don't give us heartache.

HOW WELL DO YOU KNOW YOURSELF?

Does a decision that was based on sound principles but didn't turn out perfect get you down? I've met people who plan a vacation a year in advance, making every effort to find the time of year when the weather is best, and if it turns rainy that week, they beat themselves up. They can be so torn up by it that they fret about it long after the vacation is over and wonder if they should even plan for next year's vacation. Do you see yourself as having a little of this trait in your personality?

At the risk of getting myself in trouble, I've read many surveys that say, on average, women have a higher disposition for regret than men, and younger people are more prone to regret than the old. If you fall closer to the regret side of decisions that are based on sound judgment, but they turned out wrong, it helps to remind yourself: Regret teaches lessons, but often they're the wrong lesson. It's up to you to step back and determine if it was a good decision, with a less than good result, or if there was something else you should learn from it. Feel good that you've learned and won't make it again. Then, adjust your plan and take another step forward.

It's common for people to be highly regretful and even frightened by decisions that didn't work out the way they had planned. A woman was in my office not long ago and was very upset. I'd say she was ready to give up on making decisions about her money, but she was in my office, and that was a decision by itself. Tammy is 50 years old. Six months ago, after waiting for two years, she decided to take $25,000 of long-term savings out of a money market account to buy a two-year CD. The CD paid interest of 1.40 percent, which was much higher than the 0.15 percent she had been earning for two years. Three weeks after she invested the money she saw that rates on two-year CDs went up to 1.65 percent. This upset her. She was literally telling herself that she was stupid. The good thing about Tammy is that she decided to look at herself and ask if she was the best person to be making these decisions. I suspected she would shy away from making decisions that would serve her well, so I asked her if she thought she had the inner game necessary to do what you need to. I saw she needed someone else to make these decisions for her. She hired our firm. At our next meeting I told her how important it was that she hired me as her advisor. I explained that the bigger mistake she made was keeping the money in the money market account when it could have been earning much more for the full two years, and that even 1.65 percent was a low rate relative to other contractually guaranteed investments. I feared this would upset her; instead it comforted her that her investments were now being overseen by someone who based decisions on much more suitable criteria.

WHAT IS OKAY (IF ANYTHING) FOR YOU TO LOSE?

Most people would say that it isn't okay to lose anything. The question is more related to your personal situation of risk and reward measurements. Suppose that you started with a portfolio that has a 50 percent chance of increasing your standard of living; however, this same portfolio also has a 50 percent chance of reducing by X percent your standard of living. What is the highest number X percent can be before it severely impacts you mentally? Is your answer as low as one percent, as high as 49 percent? The lower the number you chose, the more you are impacted by pain. People like Tammy don't realize that by leaving money in a money market account they are also at risk. We'll discuss inflation in another chapter, but it's clear that if Tammy could have been earning anything over 0.15 percent on her $25,000, then you can say she lost that by not being invested.

I've read surveys concluding that, on average, Americans are willing to tolerate a maximum reduction of approximately 12.5 percent. Mathematically, this says their risk tolerance is 4 to 1, (50 percent versus 12.5 percent). I believe that for most retirees this risk level is far too great, and I advise on options that keep it substantially lower.

DOES YOUR GREED CAUSE HIGH RISK?

For some, their pain comes from thinking they are missing out on something. If you were to turn on the TV and hear that stocks are up 10 percent on the year while your much safer investments earned you 5.5 percent, how upset would you be? If you felt very confident that you'd earn over 5 percent and not lose money, because you know stocks go up and down, you probably shouldn't be upset at all. Certainly not if you are retired and can't afford a loss. Yet it happens every day. Often it causes people to take money out of their more certain conservative investments and take bigger risks than they should. Know thyself—is this you?

Overconfidence is handy throughout life. But, with investing for retirement, when you can't afford a loss, but deep down tell yourself you "know" the investment will go up, or you don't want the pain of missing the gains if it does, then you may not be the right person making these decisions on your nest egg.

Here are some easy-to-understand facts that are important to completely internalize. The consistent ability to receive higher-than-average returns is extremely rare. Many investors attempting to beat the market eventually end up licking some wounds, trying to make up losses or forever hiding from investing again. If you can't completely internalize this, save yourself from agony by vetting and hiring an excellent financial advisor.

ARE YOU DETAIL-ORIENTED?

Part of knowing thyself is understanding how well you pay attention to details. Would people who know you best describe you as organized and prepared? Do you pay attention to all necessary details, or are you constantly late and missing your schedule?

How consistently you are attentive to detail can play a big part in your financial success. Do you know yourself when it comes to being detail-oriented? Here are some questions for self-analysis:

- Do you know what your investments are worth within a few thousand dollars before you open your statements?

- Do you maintain a budget for your household?

- Do you usually have a good idea how much the bill will be before it comes at a restaurant, and can you quickly figure out the tip?

- If you suffered a market loss when investing, did you learn of it when you got your statements, or were you aware as the markets lost value?

- When choosing 401(k) funds, did you use long-term and short-term performance numbers? Do you reevaluate these selections on a regular basis?

- Do you analyze an investment tip from friends or family members before you make a decision?

If you found yourself answering "yes" or "of course" to these questions, then congratulations! You should know that you are more detail-oriented than most. If you answered "no" to more than one detail-oriented question, or in some cases, you didn't even understand what the question is asking, then you may be detail oriented in some parts of your life, but that probably doesn't include your finances. This is okay, if you're aware of it. Many people who are not attentive to their investments are not because they are oriented to other details in their life. Attentive and conscientious people tend to be more successful than average. They are good at keeping their eye on the ball, but most have so many "balls" in their life they cannot retain the detail on all of them. People who are attentive are often that way because they are determined. They have higher concentration levels and are alert to many of the matters that are most important to them. They aren't superhuman, and although they may pay attention to detail in some areas of their life, or are very conscious of the impact of what they are doing, they just can't keep their eye on *all* the balls in play in their life.

These types of people will outsource many of the things they can't or don't want to focus on by hiring a professional who does.

If you can't keep your eye on the investment ball, look to hire someone to relieve you of these details.

DO OTHERS VIEW YOU AS THE LIFE OF THE PARTY?

Here is something to consider. Are you often the center of attention, gregarious, or outgoing? Do you like being the focus of the group and look forward to conversations with new people?

These questions may not seem like they have much to do with investing for retirement, but at the heart of exploring thyself, they may. People who answer yes to these questions are in the category psychologists call extroverts. Extroverts tend to be very confident, more comfortable with risk, and don't dwell on mistakes. All of these positive qualities detract from careful introspection, so these people may not listen to others and often are less honest about their own shortcomings.

Taking risk is not always a bad thing, but not taking the time to assess the affect if something goes wrong is. If you are the life of the most parties, congratulations, but force yourself to focus and assess your needs versus the risks you take with your nest egg. You should learn from your mistakes—don't ignore them, because they're often expensive. If you have tried and continue making the same mistakes, perhaps your investments should be in someone else's hands.

ARE YOU A GIVER?

When I first meet someone my immediate thoughts turn to whether I can do something for them. Not just in business, but when I meet my children's friends, people at church, and even when I meet other advisors, my radar goes up and I wonder what I can help them with. I know myself enough to be aware that something in my psychological makeup causes me to be sensitive to the needs and feelings of others. Does this sound like you? Do you make sure you make others feel at ease and determine if there is something you can do for them?

I like this trait about myself, but it can be a blessing and a curse. It's extremely important that givers know this about themselves so they can avoid saying yes when they shouldn't. Consider this example: You're a giver and you meet a person at an event who seems like a decent person. Then you find they are selling investments that you had never heard of or never considered. Rather than put up a filter trying to determine if it is a fit for you, you instead try to see how you may be able to do business with this person. It may cause you to focus more on their needs than your own, which is always bad with investment decisions. I assume everything is a scheme until I prove otherwise. If you're a giver or a pleaser, I suggest you try to adopt the same rigid fence.

ARE YOU A DREAMER?

I live in the shadows of Disney World, so I know how much people like to dream; just remember your investment portfolio is not the place for dreaming. How do you know if you're a dreamer? Are you an idea person, someone who doesn't like to follow and do things the way they've always been done? Do you find others unimaginative and slow to grasp newer ideas?

This is another very positive trait where it is important to know thyself. I've found that dreamers, or people with great imaginations, usually don't do well managing their own money. This level of intellect is better suited for ideas and inventions than money matters. Part of the reason is they become bored with routine, and the science of money management often involves routine. There are other reasons as well. When it comes to money, dreamers may fall behind because they spend their careers paying little to no attention to retirement planning. The idea of regular savings may seem too rigid or boring. They are the opposite of detail-oriented, and I've found they often have a great deal of money either left uninvested or have little saved at all.

If you are a dreamer and can't bring yourself to become more attentive to your finances, find yourself an extremely detailed oriented advisor as early in life as possible. Then make sure whatever plan you devise is implemented. Don't just dream, do!

ARE YOU A WORRIER?

Are you inclined to always question your decisions? Does negative news half a world away cause you anxiety? When you're sick, do you tend to expect the worst?

Most worriers know they are worriers. It's important that you understand this as an investor. If your investments are based on fear and a negative outlook, you'll tend to act like a deer in the headlights when it comes to your investment decisions. Remember doing nothing in a world of rising prices and longer life spans is also risky. Worrying about losing money may prevent you from even maintaining your purchasing power with the money you have.

Not to sound like a broken record, but a good strategy is to hire a competent financial advisor to design, explain, and manage your retirement investments. The advisor can explain what you hold and how it's a sensible part of your future needs. Often information and confidence that another is not worried is the perfect tonic so you can spend your time worrying about other things.

KNOW THYSELF AND KNOW OTHERS

Most market and economic models are based on the idea that we all make rational decisions to maximize our benefit. The reality is we never have perfect information to make rational decisions, and even more importantly most people don't carefully analyze all their financial decisions. Most people are emotional about spending, bet on the market based on gut feelings, and call on intuition from areas of their brain that are not tied to careful analysis or detail.

There's a field of study called behavioral economics that looks at how other human factors play a role in financial and investment decisions. Beyond what I've already discussed, there are a number of biases that are important to look for in yourself and be aware of their existence in the overall economy. These biases tend to affect market behavior and therefore are important.

- Anchoring
- Bandwagoning
- Regency bias
- Loss aversion
- Confirmation bias
- Negative or positive bias

Have you ever become attached to something and held on to it just because you've had it for so long? This is called *"Anchoring."* It could be as small as a t-shirt from a concert you went to in 1982 or a boat that just sits without being used. People also do this with information. I know many people who are still sure that a high carbohydrate diet (popular in the 1980s) is still the best diet. Science has since debunked the merits of the high carb diet. When applied to investing, anchoring refers to people who hold an investment for too long or are still making decisions on old data that has little to do with the investment's merits today.

Most people who have been around investments are aware of herd behavior or *"Bandwagoning."* Decisions in the markets are often made because "everyone else is doing it." Markets and stocks at times continue to move in price well beyond any rational analysis because the herd of buyers continues to either buy or sell because everyone else is. When an event such as a drop in interest rates occurs, people with *"Regency Bias"* will expect that rates will quickly revert back to whatever they had grown accustomed to. This perspective may have nothing to do with any factors other than their expectations of "normal." This is not a rational method in which to make investment decisions; be aware of it, so you can avoid the "noise" coming from TV announcers or even your friends who don't have their own regency bias in check.

Have you ever met someone who complains on a rainy day that it's always raining, even if it hasn't rained in days? A similar trait for investors is *"Loss-aversion bias."* These are investors who are inclined to feel losses much more than they recognize gains. So, for example, if they were to learn they have a $5,000 gain in their portfolio, they want to immediately sell because they worry the growth may not last. Their decision has nothing to do with analysis; it is based on their own set of fears.

It is very common for people in every area of their life to give more weight to the opinions of people and information that agree with their own view. This is called *"Confirmation bias,"* and I see it in my business quite a bit. For example, I'll discuss with other investment professionals the direction of the market and the economy and I will often hear them quote an economic number that suggests the market may go in one direction, even if there have been several other numbers pointing in the opposite direction. It's important to note that this bias exists for market participants and may exist in ourselves.

A *Negative or positive bias* is when the markets or individuals are inclined to place more importance on negative or positive news. This can result in important information being ignored if it doesn't conform to the bias.

The most amazing investment tool known to man still is the human brain. But it isn't perfect. Many of the lessons we've been taught that keep us out of trouble in some areas of our life could work against us when applied to our financial situation. Knowing thyself is a good start for averting these problems or deciding if you should seek the help of an advisor. You also have to consider the biases of others who participate in the various markets because whether they are right or wrong, they affect market moves and sometimes our own opinions.

SECTION 3

INCOME STRATEGIES TO LAST A LIFETIME

· 10 ·

Purpose-Driven Investing

When I made the tough decision many years ago to go into finance and then seek a path that eventually led to my becoming the CEO of my own advisory practice, it was only partially out of a desire to be my own boss. Guiding my own financial advisory firm became a quest to better serve the people who needed it most. I was still somewhat young, but I had been a practicing accountant for a while and I saw what others who called themselves financial planners were doing, or more accurately, not doing for people. In some cases I was morally outraged with what some veteran advisors and more generally, Wall Street viewed as acceptable. I also saw what many people, left to their own understanding of financial planning, were missing out on. In both cases they effectively minimized retirees' ability to earn income off their own savings. Some of the accounts were "managed" by advisors of very large investment companies. Yet I saw a flaw in their business model. People were promised an account that would get them comfortably through retirement. In many cases there is a good chance that they received the reverse of what was promised (remember the speculating airline pilot). Unfortunately, some sales professionals, particularly those at large firms, are less focused on their clients than they are at advancing themselves. I want to be careful here because I firmly believe that most advisors in our industry have their client's best interests at heart. However, with the way we are all trained to conform to the current Wall Street business model, it is very difficult for the typical advisor to shift to a true income strategy without completely going out on their own as an independent advisor.

TOP MONEY CONCERNS OF RETIREES AND PRE-RETIREES

Although I've lived the last 15 years of my adult life in the Orlando area, I have values acquired while growing up in a family with nonmaterialistic, honest parents with a great work ethic. These values present themselves in everything I do. In the early days of being an advisor, I know I benefited from this upbringing. I also fit the Mid-Atlantic state stereotype of being a good listener; it's even harder for me to not listen when someone is asking for help.

Today my office is located in Altamonte Springs, Florida, a suburb of Orlando, and I live nearby. There are about 43,000 people living in Altamonte Springs. The average age is 39.6, which is two years younger than the average for all of Florida and three years older than the whole country. As I mentioned before, statistics are deceiving. There are many children in the area, and many retirees, including widows. Whether I like it or not, being a financial advisor in Central Florida means specializing in helping people who are in, or near, retirement. As you'll see, I like it, and I wouldn't change a thing today.

The Central Florida area has well-educated residents. The area has benefited economically from a number of strengths, including many corporate headquarters, growing medical and technology industries, nearby theme parks, and all the other advantages of being a tourist destination. It's also an area where waves of Northerners flock to spend their free time during retirement in the sunshine and out of the snow.

The residents' financial concerns are probably not much different from the rest of the country. Like me, most of the people who come into my office are from someplace else. Their financial questions usually fall into four categories:

1. **Growth.** How do we achieve the maximum amount of growth in our money while minimizing the amount of risk?
2. **Income.** How do I get the highest steady income without depleting my savings?
3. **Legacy.** How do I create the most amount of legacy value to take care of my family?
4. **Liquidity.** What's the most amount of liquidity we should have in today's environment?

For most people who lived through the incredible wealth that was generated in the growth of the stock market during the 1980s and 1990s, their perception and expectation of what the stock market should provide is forever ingrained in their psyche. And it's unrealistically high. The same generations have also had their breath (along with their assets) taken away during the significant downturns. The growth we had during the good times would be great if you could count on it, but the truth is you can't and you shouldn't. If you are near retirement, you need to begin building a fortress around what you have, add as much as you can to it, and focus on safely earning as much as you can with those assets.

In Chapter 3, I discussed why the current markets may be riskier than ever, but the truth is the best retirement plans never relied on crossing your fingers and hoping for capital gains. They were always built on a steady, reliable earnings stream (cash truly is King in this context). This wisdom has not changed.

I sometimes try to make this clear at my public events by using a real estate example rather than securities or mutual funds. I find people can relate better to real estate. The concept of growth versus income is the same as any other investment.

The example scenarios I use show a choice between two different types of properties, each costing $500,000.

The first one is 250 acres about an hour's drive from Charlotte, North Carolina. On this property, from 1980 to 2010, the appraised value had an average increase of 12.27 percent per year. Parcels can be sold off individually in one-acre increments. Current price is $2,000 per acre.

The second investment choice is a small building with four residential rentals, also an hour outside of Charlotte. The tenants currently pay the owner $32,500 per year (6.5 percent of $500,000) and rents have kept pace with inflation for the past 30 years. However, the price of the property itself hasn't changed in 30 years.

A growth investor would only consider the first option. An average growth rate of 12.27 percent is appealing, whereas the 6.5 percent contractual rent agreements, with little chance of capital gains, would not seem as attractive. However, there is a lot more to consider about the growth property compared to the income property. The growth property has had extended periods where it has gone down in value 30 percent or more. It wasn't a consistent 12.27 percent year-in and year-out. From 2000 to 2010, it has averaged a rise of 1.07 percent. For a retirement plan, this growth option would be difficult for the retirees to know what value they'll have to work with in any given year. Additionally, if the land had an annual property tax of 2.27 percent (reducing the average return to 10 percent), it would increase the cost of ownership despite its absence of cash flow. This makes the actual return lower than the growth rate, and the money paid annually in order to own this property inhibits growth as well. As you'll see, this is not very different from being invested for growth in a stock mutual fund.

To pay these taxes of $11,350 due this year (even if the value declines), you'll need to sell some land. In the mutual funds case, they sell some holdings and pull it out every month for you, thereby reducing what you own. So, although an investor may be drawn in by the historic growth prospect, the cost of ownership makes it less attractive than originally thought, and there is no cash flow. So living off the vacant land would mean constantly selling your holdings until it is gone. The point is that investing for growth is speculative; most retirees cannot afford to be speculators with a majority of their savings.

The second option, the rental property, provides an earnings stream; rents will at times reset with inflation, and living off the property's yield (rent payments) does not inhibit further earnings. At the end of 30 years, if it has not appreciated one penny more than when purchased, it has fed the owner's income for 30 years. And it can continue to feed for 30 more. This is not dissimilar to income-producing securities available to investors; they can provide a predictable earnings stream without cutting into principal. If the purpose of the investment is income, then it accomplishes the goal. Keep in mind that I used a real estate rental because it is easier to understand price fluctuations not affecting income. We are all accustomed to real estate prices going up and down. Here is another analogy. Chickens continue to produce eggs as long as you don't damage the chicken. If you don't need to eat all the eggs at once, you can incubate some and grow more chickens, which increases your yield of eggs (hence, my book cover with the golden eggs). The same is true of income investing.

PURPOSE-BASED INVESTING

When I speak to retirees about the first question I hear, "How do we achieve the maximum amount of growth in our money while minimizing risk?" I generally learn what they are truly looking to accomplish. Most often, targeting growth at their life stage is not really their preference; they just weren't aware of the choices. What suits their plan is to create an earnings stream. Further, creating a "known" or contractual earnings stream provides them peace of mind not available with the risk of growth, or as I refer to it, performance investing.

The second concern listed involves income—specifically, getting the most while minimizing the impact on principal. To receive income, you must invest for income. As you know from Section 1, Wall Street, the media, and advisors barely talk about what's available. The fixed income market is actually much larger than the stock market; it's just not as hyped. I guess it's too boring. The available marketplace to the average person for income-producing alternatives flies under the radar. It's less visible in part because many of the investors are large institutions like banks, insurance companies, and other corporations. These companies are not in the business of risking capital in their investment portfolio; they have income thrown off as cash flow for other business needs. It's no wonder these institutional investors are often referred to as "the smart money."

Not unlike the growth-based real estate example, many investments—including income investments—can be laced with so many fees that by the time you are paid a return, there is nothing left. Whether you are investing in mutual funds, REITs, annuities, or any other investment product, or working with an advisor, *read everything*. Question every fee. If you aren't sure how it affects your yield, have it explained to you until you do understand. What you keep each month above your initial investment is after expenses and fees. You need to know what they are. That is the number that counts—yield to investor. This is where many investment plans can cripple earnings to the unsuspecting.

The yield that most people need coming into my office mathematically calculates to 4 to 6 percent. It has been the magic number that I find works in most cases where people were typical savers in their 401(k)s and other money they have for retirement. The expenses charged in funds, including those in your 401(k), can significantly erode what's left for you.

The rule of thumb, often from advisors and fund advice literature, is that investors should try not to pay any more than a 1.5 percent expense ratio for an equity fund. It's more likely that the average fee in a mix of funds is 1.65 percent. This is where your required yield, and the actual math of this popular savings vehicle, begins to diverge.

Let's assume you have $500,000 in a mutual fund (fees of 1.65 percent) and it has a 6 percent average growth rate for the next 15 years. In 15 years, as you move from age 55 to 70, you would pay about $200,000 in fees. This is real money! It lowers compounding yield to the mutual fund. It lowers your return for taking on the risk. The mutual fund's risk to earn 1.65 percent from you is zero, but the risk that you lose instead of gain is very real. How real? Out of the top-10 bull markets, the average correction was a decline of 20 percent in value. So probability and nearly 200 years of stock market history certainly suggests a 20 percent correction in the next few years. It could be as much as 30 to 70 percent. Let me illustrate. In order to be a realist in this illustration, I'll place that decline three years from now, after which, for the next 12 years, the 6 percent growth rate resumes.

What retirees and near-retirees should be doing to increase their income, and maximize what they get to keep, is avoid paying (in this case), nearly $200,000 over 15 years. The mutual fund it gets paid to, after all, has close to zero market risk. Financial plans instead need to turn this upside down and make sure that little or no risk is on the side of the investors, and that the investors still receive their 4 to 6 percent or more of income on investments and savings.

The third question they come into my office with is how to build a legacy. For them, it's important to either make sure a surviving spouse has no financial concerns or to provide their children with an inheritance. They have the added need to not run out of money, or additional concerns that the money should be invested in a way where it isn't consumed.

The universe of income-generating solutions can certainly be used to develop a plan throwing off 4 percent or more a year. Then after many years, they still serve to provide income without touching principal. This is important for those who want to leave a legacy. I'll mention here that you have to yield 4 percent in IRAs starting at age 70 just to break even with minimum distributions required by law. So if this legacy is to be created by passing along savings, they need to be confident they'll earn 4 percent or more.

Often times, leaving a legacy involves another financial planning tool. It may be accomplished through strategies using life insurance. This is why it's important to look at all of your financial planning together, separating investments from other assets and separating retirement goals from other goals that create inefficiencies and waste.

I should warn you that although life insurance is often compared side-by-side to savings as a legacy planning tool, it is not for the do-it-yourselfer. I've seen couples paying for years into a term policy when they would have been better served by a whole life, or universal life, policy.

Another often forgotten reason for legacy planning is fairness to surviving children. This perfect example happened recently. It involves Darek, who owns a small, local music store. Darek has an out-of-the-way store where he gives lessons and sells instruments.

It is a small store, but it sits on what is a very expensive piece of property. I was chatting with him one day about our mutual love for music and what current-day rock trends have become, and the conversation slowly turned to our kids. He's a little older than I am, and we have common ground in that he has an older son and two younger daughters. His son JJ is a young adult and works with him in the business. His daughters, although not yet adults, show no interest in the music store business. Darek wanted to make sure that his son would receive his business should something happen to him, and also how to make sure his two daughters received something of similar value. Life insurance was the perfect legacy planning solution for Darek's dilemma.

The fourth most popular question when people come into my office is about liquidity. Specifically, they want to calculate how much liquidity they'll need. For clients like Darek who have most of their wealth tied up in a business, liquidity is a big concern. For others who retire with marketable securities, it's less of a concern. If you build your retirement plan using the principles of yield, then liquidity of your holdings should not be a big concern. Surprises and emergencies are a part of life, so having access to cash in short notice is quite desirable. Most of the income-producing securities in plans I develop for the majority of retirees are readily marketable. A sale will show up in your account within three trading days.

BEATING THE DRUM

Financial planning and investing is a necessary part of life. You lose purchasing power if you don't plan, and plan correctly.

The 4 to 6 percent yield, as discussed, was derived using the history of inflation rates, the average account size of middle-class retirees, distributions to them, and anticipated expenses (i.e., new car purchase) over a 30-year period. I didn't just randomly pick this magic number, and more importantly, it would be useless information if it wasn't available in today's market.

When you're in or near retirement, investing for yield, and making sure you won't lose purchasing power, this is the best way to begin to develop your plan. This is not a new approach; I've been creating plans with this idea with great results, and in crazy markets, for a long time. My clients are purpose-based investors; they get to relax when they hear about all the volatility because their income remains consistent and predictable as a result of their plan. While my clients aren't swinging for the fences, we are regularly providing singles and doubles and sometimes triples, season after season. I'm proud of providing this level of foresight. It alleviates the biggest nightmare that sets folks' radars off. They get to avoid the sleepless nights wondering when the stock market will fall and how it will affect their assets. They're relieved to know they have a choice. And if they choose investing for yield with the universe of income-generating solutions, it's a win/win for them. This is very important for most retirees and pre-retirees, but it's significantly downplayed in the advertising world, the news world, and the financial planning arena. I don't necessarily get my kicks out of beating the same old "yield" drum to them, but if that's what I have to do to actually help folks and sharpen their focus on assets that will best serve their needs in retirement, then I'll keep the beat going.

· 11 ·

The Common Sense Approach

When I meet with older Americans, who have been around the
block a few times, I can state with certainty that they don't care
how much I know until they know how much I care. My common
sense approach to income strategies is a good first indicator to how
much I care. It provides the answer to the many concerns they have
with other options, and solves other headaches they didn't know
they might catch.

DEFINING UNCOMMON SENSE

Since the early 2000s, retirees' portfolios have been failing to provide growth and security suitable to provide them with the money
and reliability appropriate for retirement living.

The 50-year-old who invested in the stock market in the summer of 2000 and expected to retire at 65 may have had to let that
birthday pass and continue working. If they got back to even seven
years later, they were violently derailed again by the stock market.

As of late 2016, they earned just 2 percent per year in stocks. The expected return they counted on for them to retire may have been between 8 and 13 percent. That's quite a difference. What's even worse, during that period where they had roller-coaster ups and downs when they averaged just 2 percent, the cumulative inflation rate was over 39 percent.

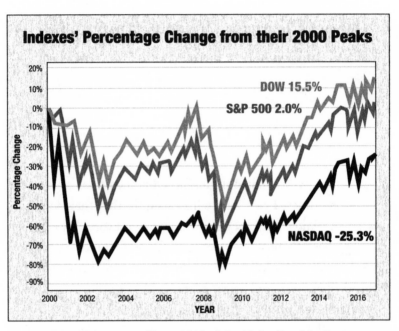

Price Movements Since 2000 of the Major Stock Indices.
When you look at how close stock prices are to their starting point of
the year 2000, it is easy to see that this asset class cannot be relied
upon for financial planning in retirement.

There is no expectation that stocks begin to soar; in fact, as mentioned in earlier chapters, price-earnings ratios and normal ebbs and flows of stock market prices argue for a steep sell-off in the next few years.

Discarding 401(k) statements without looking at them is what so-called experts advise many investors to do. The uncommon sense reasoning parroted by these "experts" is that you should buy and hold—and you should always invest in the stock market. The stock market, they say, "always goes up over time." So they tell clients not to be detail-oriented because looking at statements can only cause you to make an emotional decision (such as not to hold, or perhaps to get a different advisor).

Mutual fund companies are part of those trumpeting this self-serving advice to their customers. They spend a lot of advertising dollars convincing people to buy and hold—in other words, there is no reason to open your statements. They want you to own stocks or stock funds, hold them for a very long period, and not let market swings bother you. Is covering your eyes really the best advice for anyone over age 45? How about if you're over 65 and were looking forward to an increase in account size for living expenses? What they repeat all too often just isn't a sensible strategy.

IS IT COMMON SENSE TO TELL A 65-YEAR-OLD TO WAIT OUT A 35-YEAR CYCLE?

What if you don't have long before you need to use your money? What if you're a member of the group of investors who can't wait 7 to 10 years to recover from natural downturns of the stock market? This is generally the case for most retiring investors.

If you're part of the group with 20 years or less until retirement age, you've had to lick some serious investment wounds many times. If the stock market behaves in accordance with its long- and short-term historic cycles, it's going to take an even greater toll soon. This time, you're older and don't have the extra years it takes to recover from a sharp drop or prolonged sell-off. I ask my clients if they'd be willing to forever scale down and rewrite how they intend to live out these years. The question is generally met with a face of disgust. I agree with their nonverbal answer, and I continue to define how deep the uncommon sense runs.

The financial needs of Baby Boomers and those right behind them are not being addressed. There are an estimated 123.5 million people in this group and they've been ignored by Wall Street, mutual funds, the brokerage community, and certainly Washington. In fact, even friendly financial advisors have not yet awakened to the idea that the advice they're giving is just parroting Wall Street. The story Wall Street wants you to accept just does not serve you well, because it doesn't make sense. The truth is it could even cost an enormous chunk of your assets and personal security.

MAKING SENSE OF THE SITUATION

I've built a thriving practice by offering a more secure, less stressful, and perhaps even more lucrative method of providing for yourself in retirement. I would have expected many others to follow, but without the support of the media and other information outlets, I understand why they don't. I can tell you firsthand, it's not always easy maintaining your integrity by telling a different story. Even if every aspect of what you say is true, verifiable, and based on common sense.

I've even made some inroads into being that support and education that others need. Go to my website at www.FellowshipFinancial.com and click on the "news". Listen to what I have spoken about over on CNBC and Fox Business News and in my radio show, "The Retirement Income Doctor." Look at the title of the book in your hand, which is published by Advisor's Academy Press and distributed by Simon and Shuster. I'm not just out to help my clients, I'm out to start an income revolution by getting the word out. There are sound strategies, there are answers.

INVESTING IN STOCKS
ISN'T COMPLETELY SENSELESS

Maybe we can see why they want you to invest in stocks if we look at what the stock market is. It's really just a marketplace. At the marketplace bids and offers are satisfied in what essentially can be viewed as an auction of partial ownership in certificates of corporations. Prices or these stock certificates don't necessarily reflect corporate profits or even future earnings. After all, it's buyers and sellers who set prices, and they are driven by speculation, emotions, and cycles of economic activity. They're also heavily affected by investors who believe they can make more (greed) or investors who decide to get out before they've lost money (fear).

The stock markets are also driven more and more by nonhuman computer trading, based on complex math decision models. These models, if triggered at the same time, can make portfolio-crushing changes in the blink of an eye. Even the most seasoned market veteran isn't prepared to understand this speed-of-light environment.

Where are you in all this? If you're like my clients, you can't fail if you want to ever retire. As the saying goes, "Failure is not an option." Most of my clients had never been shown the tools they need to succeed prior to us working with them. The knowledge base of most Boomers comes from what they read in finance magazines, the business section of the news, paid-for advertisements, or investment television shows whose purpose is to sell advertising space.

Selling ad space to companies selling investment products can get in the way of unbiased reporting; it can even affect what strategies are reported to you and, more importantly, which are not.

NOT ALL FINANCIAL ADVISORS HAVE SEEN THE LIGHT

As advisors go, I'm definitely a different drummer. I have come to the business from a unique angle compared to most others, my focus on the client's best interest is always number one, and I dig and research and partner with other advisors and portfolio managers for the best solutions and workable strategies. As for so many others, it probably comes as no surprise this late in the book that financial advisors get their information from the same places most people do. For the advisors who say something outside of conventional wisdom and Wall Street axioms, they find that their potential for business growth shrinks. Especially if what they're explaining is completely foreign to their audience. Unless they're very good at shouting their message above the noise of every other outlet, they grow slowly while watching the business of mainstream planners swell. I am breaking this trend, and I am personally delivering copies of *Common Sense Income Strategies* to some financial advisors.

I've never been an advisor who can just blame any damage on the market. There are advisors who blame the market and not themselves. They get away with it, too. They've learned that they can just tell their clients, "It's the market's fault," and then advise, "Buy and hold; the market always goes up," which bails you both out. That is, it bails you out if you can wait that long.

Baby Boomers are a large group of Americans who still take responsibility for themselves. If there's a problem, they don't wait for anyone to fix it for them. They figure out what they need to do, and they do whatever it takes. The most notable characteristic I can think of regarding older people today is they proudly survive and thrive.

If you're in the age group that's 55 and older, you're likely to have more of a challenge retiring than your parents did. If you've done everything "right"—that is, everything you've been told is a must—you may even be wondering how you could even consider retiring. The reasons are many. Frankly, most are out of your control. They include challenges like low interest rates, corporate retirement plan changes, and a dangerous real estate, stock, and commodities market. Some of the difficulties were even forced on you through government regulation; others came about by hearing half-truths repeated so many times by Wall Street and the financial news outlets that you could not help but believe them. There's one other challenge that you didn't count on—you're expected to live much, much longer.

You shouldn't worry if you feel you haven't yet met these many challenges, but you should make sure you're implementing an informed and smart plan. One of the traits people in this age group can be most proud of is their ability to get the job done. They are incredibly resilient. I sometimes joke that it's this tenacity that raised longevity expectations, rather than medicine.

We've gained experience having lived through difficult times with a huge number of peers. Survived competing for everything from teacher's attention in swollen class rooms to jobs, and have beaten the next guy in bidding on a home.

If you're 55 and older, you're partially inoculated to austerity, recession, high unemployment, and high inflation. After all, you lived through the "stagflation" of the 1970s, when it seemed that from the end of the Vietnam War through Nixon's resignation, and even during the high interest rates and weak economy of the Carter years, that there was very little good news.

You probably had parents who invested very little in stocks back then. For our parents, giving us a U.S. Savings Bond as a gift *was* investing.

You also saw the country survive the 1970s, which ended with double-digit inflation and double-digit unemployment. Then, experienced what once seemed impossible—the end of the Soviet Union and the Cold War. Many of us became adults in the 1980s and finally enjoyed a reigniting of national pride and economic growth that just a few years earlier was thought to have been lost forever. It wasn't, and your retirement hopes aren't, either.

If you're 55 years old or more, you're in the home stretch to retirement and have to protect what you have and set your money up in a way where it's clearly working for you. Mostly, you need to know what to expect from your investments, and you can't do that if you don't know what value they will offer you after you become invested.

Large finance companies like banks and insurance companies also need to calculate what to expect on their investments. The investments have a purpose. Institutions develop an investment policy that meets that purpose. They hire internal portfolio managers and research analysts with top-tier experience and education and provide them with state-of-the-art analytical tools, access to markets, and research capabilities.

SHOULDN'T RETIRES AND NEAR-RETIREES TAKE THE SAME STEPS?

The institutions have no commercial reason to show anyone that they stack all the odds in their favor, and then they have one more unheralded method that almost ensures certainty of outcome.

It's not difficult to implement the proven method that the aptly named "smart money" uses regularly. You just have to know about it. But most people don't know about this important method. As I said, most Americans were instructed on how to invest by advertisements, magazines, and television shows that get paid by those advertisers.

The big banks, insurance companies, and corporate America using this method have no reason to talk about it. In fact, these are among the brightest guys in money management; they don't invest client money, they invest the money of huge financial entities including JP Morgan, TD Bank, and Goldman Sachs. They quietly do their job with confidence, and gladly let someone who knows much less than they do spout off on TV or in magazines. Their job is to make sure the company they invest money for can, for example, exceed its budget.

They aren't trying to sell anyone anything, so sitting at their modest desk with state-of-the-art analytical tools is the best use of their time. In fact, most people aren't aware that investing in stocks is considered too risky for most portfolios of cities, states, and counties. Government entities prohibit it with their own money. They view it as so risky that it's expressly prohibited in most cases. Instead, municipalities have a list of acceptable investments. The list varies from state to state, but is similar to the institutional list guiding banks, insurance companies, and much of corporate America.

It contains high-grade, fixed income securities. That is, income-generating alternatives are acceptable government investments, where stocks typically aren't.

Here are some common sense steps you can take to begin down the road to a sound income strategy:

- If you can't afford to lose money in the stock market, don't own any stocks.

- Find an advisor who specializes in income-generating investments. If you're in the Central Florida area, contact my office; if you are outside of Florida, call or email my office and I will try to find a suitable fit for your needs.

- Determine your investment strengths and weaknesses from Chapter 9.

- Review the Seven Pillars of Wealth in Chapter 8 regularly. They will help with many noninvestment financial matters.

- Lastly, if you're going to have your investments managed with the prudence and common sense of an institution, you must learn to view your holdings as they do. Remember, the issuer is contractually obligated to pay you the principal at maturity and ignore interim price swings.

HOLD TO MATURITY (HTM)

There is an accounting designation that banks, insurance companies, corporations, and other institutions use when they invest in debt instruments for their known return. Any variations in market price during the holding period are considered noise. After all, they are receiving exactly what they contracted for. The HTM designation tells their CPAs not to pay attention to price swings. This can be harder for individual investors who are taught to look at value changes in non-maturing investments like stocks and mutual funds. Accounting standards tell institutions it's perfectly okay to view it at cost. I know my clients will be able to take their emotions out of the way if their securities drop below the purchase price before maturing.

COMMON SENSE

I recognize this strategy of purpose-driven investing is different from the pie chart of asset allocation that you're accustomed to seeing and hearing about. That more familiar strategy isn't likely to suit your purpose if you're in or near retirement. The purpose-driven strategy is very likely a better fit.

· 12 ·

The World of
Income-Generating Investments

Most financial service and investment firms recognize three basic categories of investments: conservative, moderate, and aggressive.

The investments that have come to be categorized as aggressive are those investors usually turn to for growth and capital appreciation. As the table shows, they include things such as common stock, stock mutual funds, speculative real estate, and commodities. I'll make the point again that these investments are typically owned in hopes of receiving capital appreciation, not income. They're considered "aggressive" in part because they are viewed as riskier: It's a given that sometimes when you invest for gains you get losses instead—or that reaching for growth can have more detrimental consequences than when investing in the other categories.

Categories of Investment Risk

CONSERVATIVE	MODERATE	AGGRESSIVE
Certificate of Deposit	Corporate Bonds	Common Stocks
Government Bonds	Indexed Annuities	Stock Mutual Funds
Fixed Annuities	Preferred Stock	Commodities
Insured Municipal Bonds	R.E.I.T.s	"Speculative" Real Estate
	BDCs	

The table breaks out the different asset classes within each category, but I'll define them at a 10,000-foot level so as to help with the material coming later in the chapter.

On the other side of the spectrum are instruments that are considered "conservative" because they, by most standards, are deemed to have no or extremely low default risk. Conservative investments include bank CDs, government bonds, fixed annuities, and insured municipal bonds. In the middle are "moderate" instruments that have some default risk but are generally considered to have a much lower risk of loss than aggressive investments. These moderate options include non-insured municipal bonds, corporate bonds, indexed annuities, preferred stock, and Real Estate Investment Trusts (REITs) and Business Development Companies (BDCs). The instruments on the left and in the middle of the table have two things in common:

1. They're considered, to some degree, to have less risk of loss than the investments in the aggressive category.

2. They are instruments that people invest in primarily for income. In other words, they are not investments that people typically invest in first with growth in mind, although they can appreciate in value. The interest and dividends that are typically earned by the vehicles on the left and the middle of the table represent a means for investors to generate reliable income, as well as a way for them to grow their money reliably through the reinvestment of the interest and dividends paid at regular intervals. (Remember Chapter 10: incubating the eggs to produce more chickens that produce more eggs).

It's this bird-in-the-hand reliability that makes them popular with retirees, once they understand them. When looking to reliably know what to expect year in and year out, crossing your fingers and hoping for growth and capital appreciation is no match for receiving regular income strategically with reliable income.

BOND MUTUAL FUNDS

Before we move away from this table, I want to point out that there are bonds in the conservative column and higher levels of default risk bonds in the moderate column, but I have not listed bond funds. Most advisors would list them in the moderate category with corporate bonds, and I believe their behavior is more like stock mutual funds, so I am offering an explanation as to why and will let you decide who is right.

YOU DECIDE

Generally, investors who invest in bonds look at two main ways of investing in them. They can invest in bonds outright or they can invest in bond funds that hold a portfolio of bonds. When investors buy an individual bond, they have two important guarantees: a fixed rate of interest for the life of the bond, and the return of the face value when it matures. Both guarantees obviously assume that there have been no defaults. With that assumption, the investors know exactly what they are going to earn on the individual bond when held to maturity.

By comparison, bond funds are investment companies that own individual bonds. There is no maturity date and no guarantee of principal payments. The value of the underlying bonds can go up or down in value and depending on when you want to receive a distribution, you may have suffered a capital loss. That's right—just like stock funds, there is no maturity date and no return of principal at maturity. This is why I categorize bond funds in the same category as stock mutual funds. Their ability to serve retirees or other investors isn't much better.

They give investors a false sense of security. It simply means that when the stock market drops by 40 percent, your bond funds may only lose 25 percent. They will lose less, yes, but they will still lose. If you need to draw income when the value is down, you will have to sell more of your principal to receive the same amount of income as when the value was higher. This is true of mutual funds as well and can be quite harmful to your investments.

That's important because many factors can cause bonds and bond mutual funds to fluctuate while you hold them. Most people have heard that when interest rates go down, bond values tend to go up, and vice versa. That's really an oversimplification and just one of the many factors that can impact bond prices during their lifetime.

With all that in mind, imagine that you are a client of an advisor who specializes in individual bonds while your friend Joe is with an advisor who's put him in bond mutual funds. If something happens in the bond market to cause bond values to drop, a portfolio of individually held bonds and a bond mutual fund might drop similar amounts in value, but because you're in individual bonds, yours is only a paper loss. If you choose to hold those bonds in your portfolio to maturity, then, as noted, you will get your face value back at that time—again, assuming there have been no defaults. But for Joe, who has the mutual funds, he may experience an actual loss, not just a paper loss. In other words, a loss that might have been only a temporary paper loss in individual bonds can turn out to be an actual monetary loss in bond funds.

Since that's the case, you might wonder why so many financial advisors use bond mutual funds instead of individual bonds. One possibility is that the majority of advisors today specialize in growth-oriented, stock market–based strategies: those things in the "aggressive" column. Advisors who specialize in the stock market or the growth side are often not very proficient at fixed income analysis, which is very different. Therefore, it's easier for those advisors to recommend a bond mutual fund than a portfolio of individual bonds because, in so doing, they are leaning on the fund manager to pick the individual bonds. Bond funds really are a simpler way for stock market–based advisors or even do-it-yourselfers to invest in the bond market. Like most things in life, simplicity comes at a cost, and in this case that cost is exposing yourself to significantly more risk with bond mutual funds than you would with a portfolio of individual bonds.

VARIABLES TO CONSIDER

Returning to the table of asset classes, understand that if you are investing in the different categories of individual bonds or even preferred stocks, there are many variables to consider. First is the creditworthiness of the issuer. The higher the issuer's credit rating, the lower the interest or dividend rate; the lower the credit rating, the higher the interest or dividend rate. In the case of municipal bonds, you also need to understand how your marginal tax bracket has an effect on your decision. The next thing you need to consider is the maturity date, but at the same time you also want to look at the yield curve to see where you get the most bang for your buck.

Then you also need to consider the yields offered on various types of fixed income securities. There are at least four different types of quoted interest rates that all mean different things, which means you need to understand such things as an individual securi-ty's coupon rate, current yield, yield to maturity, and yield to call—as well as whether a bond is callable or noncallable, or convertible or nonconvertible.

This is all just an overview, and I hope it gives you a sense of why I strongly suggest working with a qualified advisor who specializes in fixed income instruments if you have no, or even limited, real-world experience with such instruments yourself. In other words, don't try this at home. You can probably also understand better why many stock market–based advisors prefer to "keep it simple" by working with bond funds. You may also be wondering about the wisdom of buying bonds in today's market with interest rates so low, thinking that when interest rates go back up, bonds will invariably drop in value. Your concerns are probably based to a large extent on the fact that many stock market–based advisors and Wall Street firms have been actively promoting that very mes-sage. I believe this focus on a "bond bubble" is primarily a scare tactic being used in an effort to keep investors from moving out of the stock market and into bonds. As explained, if you plan to hold bonds to maturity, then a price swing caused by interest rates be-come largely a moot point, in addition to which—as I've also ex-plained—there are many factors that impact bond values besides interest rates.

To elaborate, one such factor is risk premium. When interest rates go up, it's because the economy is doing well and investors are becoming more confident. At that time, they typically require a lower risk premium, which means less additional interest to go from government bonds to corporate bonds. What that does is partially offset the negative effects to bond values of increasing interest rates. Further, by creating a portfolio of bonds with staggered maturity dates, or laddering, you will be able to step up with interest rates over time.

WHAT ABOUT ANNUITIES?

Returning to the table of asset classes, I want to look briefly at annuities. Odds are you already know these can be extremely complicated investment tools. Some have embedded fees and some have no fees at all. Some are subject to market volatility, and some have zero volatility risk. Some are irrevocable and others more flexible. In fact, there are so many factors to consider with annuities that unless you have real-world experience with the various types of annuities, you certainly shouldn't pursue this option without the help of a qualified specialist in income-generating investment strategies.

Preferred Stocks:

Preferred stocks, which trade like equities, are a separate class of stock that is purchased primarily for the dividend income it produces. The variables mentioned earlier apply to preferred stocks as well. There are hundreds of preferred stocks in a variety of industries with various characteristics and risk levels. So, once again it is important that you work with an advisor who specializes in these types of securities, and can guide you in the selection process.

REITs/BDCs

Regarding REITs, the options are also extremely varied. When choosing REITs, one needs to look at the type of real estate that the REIT is invested in, the average length of the leases within the REIT, and the profile of the major tenants, cash flow, dividend coverage, as well many other factors. Simply put, REITs are every bit as varied and complex in their own way as annuities. It's important to know if it's an equity REIT or Mortgage REIT.

A BDC (Business Development Company) acts as a middle market lender to mostly American privately held companies. BDCs can be varied in their strategies, structure, and portfolio characteristics. It is very important to understand the differences in order to identify the strongest candidates for your portfolio. It is important to know how the BDC is managed; the BDC's cash flow and dividend coverage are also important facts to consider. Both REITs and BDCs can be either publicly traded or non-public, and each has its merits and risks. Both types can provide a solid stream of reliable income.

DULL, BORING, AND OLD-FASHIONED

More than 30 years ago, conservative financial investment alternatives were extremely popular with retirees and those approaching retirement because of their income orientation. Since the last bull market of the 1980s and 1990s, however, when investors became addicted to the stock market, they have gotten labeled as "dull, boring, or old-fashioned." As a result, most investors today have, at best, a basic understanding of these investment strategies without any real-world experience. A good, experienced advisor who specializes in these income-generating alternatives can guide you through an educational process and help you understand the pros and cons of each: their risks, expected returns, and how they may or may not fit with your personal situation and objectives.

With the exception of bank certificates of deposit (CDs), all of the conservative-to-moderate investment vehicles I've discussed are designed to generate reasonable returns in today's low interest rate environment. They are generally considered to have less risk of loss than common stocks or stock mutual funds. Again, building your wealth by receiving predictable interest and dividends from your investments is what I call a "bird in the hand" approach, and a smarter alternative in today's environment than crossing your fingers and toes and hoping for capital gains—which, as noted, can quickly become losses.

WHAT IF THERE IS A BOND BUBBLE?

There is no question that the Federal Reserve holding down rates through quantitative easing could create a bond market bubble that may not end smoothly for some investors. After all, interest rates have been held to historically low levels for years, with the Fed notching up rates when it sees economic strength can support it. It's also a fact that rates have much more room to move up than down. As mentioned earlier, rate increases mathematically reduce the value of bonds. Holders of bonds who invested to take advantage of predictable, steady interest rate payments, along with a known maturity date, shouldn't worry about any decline in market value. *If they're holding to maturity, bondholders can generally expect to receive "the face value of the bond at maturity. (barring unforeseen events)."*

WHAT A RATE RISE MEANS FOR A BOND MUTUAL FUND OR ETF

As rates rise, investors in bond funds and bond Exchange Traded Funds (ETFs) will see their portfolio value diminish. Therefore I don't invest my clients in bond funds. Since the fund can't mature, investors have to either watch the value plummet or they can sell at a capital loss. When rates rise, bond funds likely won't have the option to wait until a set maturity date; the holder of individual bonds generally will have that option. For bond ETF investors, the loss will be the difference between their purchase price and their sale price. For bond mutual fund investors it could be much worse—they may have this loss and a huge tax bill on top of it. This adds insult to injury.

Investors in bond mutual funds pay taxes each year on capital gains incurred by the trading of securities within the fund itself. If the fund manager purchases a bond for the fund and interest rates later decline, the value of that holding increases. Over the past 10 years rates have continued to decline. This means almost all holdings in bond funds are above the cost of purchase (unrealized gain). When rates begin to go up (prices down), investors are likely to seek shelter by stampeding out of their bond funds. The fund manager will often be forced to sell bonds to cover the redemptions. By selling, they will book capital gains and create a tax bill for those left in the fund. This is when bond funds can get very ugly. Recent investors in the fund will have lower asset values, yet whether they sell or not, they are responsible to pay taxes on the fund's capital gains. The fund will most likely be taking capital gains, even if the individual investor is down in value. This is especially problematic where the bond fund's holdings were purchased years ago when rates were higher (prices lower).

INCOME WITHOUT CASH FLOW

How would you like a tax event without any cash flow to cover it? If you hold a bond mutual fund you may have this experience.

This is because coupon payments are tax events to holders in mutual funds. Investors with nonqualified money in a taxable bond mutual fund (not municipal) will be required to pay tax on coupon interest payments at their "ordinary income" rate. Unless investors sell shares in the fund, they can expect a cash outflow (taxes) without any offsetting cash inflow on their holdings. To explain it another way: The bonds held by a bond mutual fund pay coupon interest. The interest is paid (typically retained in the fund but credited to the fund's investors) as a monthly dividend. This is taxed the same as when an investor holds an individual bond directly; the "interest dividend" payments are taxed at the investor's ordinary income rate. The big difference is that an investor is paid the coupon cash from an individual bond, which will help with the tax increase it generates. If the coupon cash is credited to a bond fund, the investor will often be paying the tax burden out of pocket. If the bonds are tax-exempt municipal bonds, the coupon interest of the individual bond and the interest dividend credited to a mutual fund is not taxed—if set up correctly, that is. However, municipal bond funds can have taxable capital gains, which surprises many people who thought that those funds don't generate taxable events.

ONE MORE REASON TO OWN INDIVIDUAL BONDS AND NOT FUNDS

If you are working with a financial advisor who insists that you get your bond market exposure through bond mutual funds, hit them with this tidbit that CPA financial advisors are keenly aware of, and may have escaped the notice of others.

Not all mutual funds are managed for maximum earnings. Many are traded with the idea that a more attractive offering is a fund that minimizes taxes and other costs to the investor. There are fixed income mutual funds that are more tax-efficient and seek to match winning trades with losing trades for a capital gains/capital loss tax offset. They will also avoid high numbers of trades with the objective of avoiding high short-term capital gains taxes. Mutual funds all have different cost structures and associated fees. The average expense ratio of bond mutual funds is currently 0.65 percent (according to Investment Company Institute and Lipper). If the weighted average yield of the underlying bonds is 3.25 percent, then the fund's expense ratio alone reduces this yield by 20 percent. The typical investment grade, medium-term bond fund today has a weighted average yield of 2.50 percent. Reduce that by 0.65 percent in expenses and more than a quarter of the fund's yield is being reduced by expenses.

YOUR TAKEAWAY

Knowing what you will earn by investing in income-producing instruments with set, contractual maturities makes retirement much easier, as compared to investing in stocks that go up and down and bond mutual funds that don't provide an income stream, as well as also going up and down.

A custom-tailored, income-producing portfolio is the best answer for most retirees. Individual bonds can have an important place in this portfolio, and should be created by someone who has the tools and the know-how.

Customization is worth a lot. Everyone has a different set of investment needs. Building a portfolio of bonds that are tailored to meet a household's circumstance can be quite beneficial. A few years ago it was common for people with large capital losses on property sales to look to offset them with gains. Many looked to the gains in individual bonds as the best tax strategy. The opposite can also be true for investors with capital gains elsewhere, by offsetting with bonds, which have declined in valuation. Individuals who are looking for a fixed stream of income to cover known living expenses ought to consider individual noncallable bonds with regular coupon payments. For example, a portfolio of these bonds with coupon payments may help meet regular cash flow needs. Many have more paid during months when they expect they'll have a larger expense. ETFs won't provide this option and a bond fund won't deliver that level of precision.

ARE YOU SURPRISED YOU HAVEN'T HEARD THIS BEFORE?

Perhaps the large mutual fund companies that advertise heavily in magazines and on TV don't want you to know. I've met many advisors who say they've diversified their clients into bonds using funds. They didn't know the interest rate risk and tax consequence between individual bond ownership and bond funds can be dramatic. They may simply lean heavily on the fund management and diversification within a bond fund without considering the risks mentioned here.

· 13 ·

Interest Rates, CDs, and Annuities/Inflation

Earning above the rate of inflation should be one of your top priorities in retirement. This chapter probably should come with the disclaimer: "Don't try this at home," but since you've already read Chapter 9 ("Know Thyself"), you should now have more securities and investment instrument information whether you wish to speak to an advisor at a very informed level or do it yourself. The instruments I am about to list aren't all buy suggestions, but they are included here so you may understand what you're avoiding as well as what you may wind up benefiting from.

BEYOND THE NEED FOR INCOME

There are many considerations in addition to annual income that are weighed in the balance when you implement a common sense income strategy. These other inputs to the ultimate strategy include how long you need your funds to last, liquidity needs and expectations, expected rate of interest paid, payment schedule, and risk tolerance.

Annuities: may often be part of the solution. They can provide stable income, guaranteed lifetime payments, and a high level of financial security.

Annuities are certainly not the only product in the fixed income strategy toolbox. There is always more than one way to accomplish a goal and diversification across asset classes is an important aspect of success. When devising a strategy by yourself or with a financial planner, there are additional options you may want to use.

Bonds: are another staple of income planning in retirement, especially corporate and municipal bonds. They can help meet a retiree's investment goals in many unique ways. Individual corporate bonds (which can be viewed as legal IOUs) typically pay interest twice a year, each time at half their stated interest rate. For example, a 6 percent bond will pay you 3 percent at six-month intervals. When held to maturity, the bond pays you the par (or stated) value. It's easy to see how bonds can be used to develop an income stream. Often investors try to schedule higher interest payments at times of the year when their expenses are up (e.g., when property taxes are due) and lower payments when their expenses are lower.

State and local governments also issue bonds called municipal bonds, or just munis. Retirees in high tax brackets or in high tax states often own munis in their portfolios. This is because interest payments on these bonds is often exempt from federal income tax. One of the characteristics of a municipal bond is a lower interest payment than a similarly rated corporate bond. If you are not in one of the highest income tax brackets, muni bonds may not make sense for you.

In addition to trying to schedule interest payments according to your cash needs, scheduling maturities can have a big impact on your long-term results. If rates are rising it may make sense to have maturities shorter in order to capture increases in rates when the maturities are reinvested. It's important to calculate the breakeven investment rate necessary and weigh it against expectations. This is because interest rates on bonds are typically already higher on bonds with longer maturities. One way investors develop a bond portfolio that will adapt to changing rates and provide liquidity is what they call "laddering." Laddering is buying bonds with maturities that continue to step out over a period of time. Over time, when each matures, its proceeds can be reinvested. If bond yields have risen the portfolio benefits from higher interest rates.

Certificates of Deposit (CDs): Yes, CDs—are viewed as an income-generating alternative. If you've ever owned a CD you can appreciate the joy of knowing exactly what you are going to receive. They offer a fixed interest rate for a set term and, like bonds, typically will pay you interest at scheduled payment dates.

Retiring is not necessarily a reason to completely turn your back on growth-orientated investments, though they may involve greater volatility. Remember, past performance does not guarantee future results.

Common stocks: offering steady dividends are of course subject to the company's performance and not contractually guaranteed, but they can straddle the fence for investors who can live with some unknowns in order to potentially capitalize on price fluctuations of a non-maturing security.

Preferred stocks: are different from common stocks. The dividend rate is set at issuance and these dividends are paid before any dividend is available for common stockholders. Any dividends not paid, in many cases, are required to be caught up in the future before any common dividends are paid as well. The fixed payment creates a situation where prices of preferred stocks tend to behave somewhat like bonds. An important difference between the two is that preferred stocks don't mature. Preferred shares usually pay a higher dividend rate than common shares.

Treasury Inflation-Protected Securities (TIPS): pay a lower fixed interest rate than traditional Treasuries. However, the principal owned and received at maturity (or sale) is automatically adjusted upward twice a year to match changes in inflation as measured by the consumer price index (CPI). Your interest payments are then calculated on the increased (inflation adjusted) amount. One drawback of TIPS is that federal taxes on increases in your principal, along with interest payments, are collected each year, despite not having received a cash payment for the inflation adjustment.

Depending on your needs and the state of the market for any of these alternatives, a combination of carefully blended, then regularly monitored securities, investments, and annuities may be used to develop a sound income strategy that provides for income in your retirement account.

· 14 ·

Front-Burner Things to Do Now

If you're within 5 to 10 years of retirement, you are in the retirement "red zone" and there are a number of things you should begin to do. Even if retirement is more than 10 years away for you, these common sense steps can still apply to your situation. First among them is determine if you are on track for retirement. To the best extent possible, begin to know your numbers. What are your expected costs? What is your necessary income? How much will come from Social Security? Will you be able to roll your retirement accounts to take advantage of income opportunities?

You may be able to do seat-of-the-pants calculations, but I'm suggesting that you sit down with your records, grab a sheet of paper along with anything else that could be affected by the plan, and make certain you haven't forgotten anything. Don't assume you know what another significant person in your household expects either; you want the surprises now while you can make necessary alterations to your plan.

The overall goal is to determine which decisions are best regarding taking Social Security, your current asset allocations, and if married, if you are going to be staggering your retirements. Another question that will have to be answered, for example, if you have a pension plan, will you be taking one lifetime or two?

You'll also want to determine if your costs are going to fall in retirement or if they may rise. One of the big factors for many in retirement is healthcare coverage and what your needs will be.

Fortunately, in retirement many costs go down. Remember Chapter 5 on "Retirement Life"? I gave you some government statistics on how retirees experience much lower costs in some areas after they leave work. Sharpen your pencil (and check your senior discounts) because it's time for you to determine what costs will be reduced and which will rise. I also suggest using Murphy's Law as a guide: whatever can go wrong, will go wrong. This way your calculations are conservative and you're less likely to be caught short down the road.

What I generally do with people looking to retire is make two lists: one for costs that they expect to remain the same and another for those costs they expect to change in one direction or the other. Within each category there could be quite a breakdown as well. Then I look for all sources of savings and income. Once we know the expected costs, we calculate the known income expected. There is typically a gap between the known income and the expected costs. This is where common sense income investments are used. Calculate how large the savings for retirement will be at the age you expect to retire, then using your shortfall, a simple division equation calculates the yield (interest rate) necessary to fill that gap. For help, refer back to Chapter 11. If the gap is too large for the interest rate environment, you may have to plan to make some adjustments. These adjustments could include saving more now, reducing planned expenditures in retirement, or working part-time in retirement, etc.

Gap Calculation:

Social Security + Pension = X

Annual Costs of all Expenses = Y

All assets that can earn income at retirement = Resources

X (minus) Y = GAP

GAP / Resources = Required Yield

A formula to calculate the necessary yield (interest rate) needed to cover the shortfall between your savings and income if you want to leave the principal untouched.

Here is a list of costs to consider. Use it as a guide:

- **Housing expenses.** Will you be living in your current home? Do you anticipate your electric bill to increase? If you have a mortgage, how much longer until the mortgage is paid off? If the mortgage is variable rate, is it going to rise? Will you be able to maintain the yard or have to hire someone? Are upgrades or repairs planned for your home? Do your taxes generally rise each year? Housing costs are generally fixed, but it's important to evaluate any possible scenarios related to your home and account for repairs and maintenance.

- **Medical insurance.** Most company-sponsored plans are no longer transferable. What will your insurance costs be, and when will you be eligible for a medigap policy?

- **Costs for dependents.** Will you have dependents for whom you're responsible? Calculate what the expected costs will be. You may want to include pets in this section as well.

Don't forget that if you plan to travel, caring for these "dependents" may add to their costs.

- **Entertainment and travel expenses.** For some people, these might decline precipitously; for others, they might be far higher. This is why you have to have this conversation with all who are involved. This is the time to learn if your retirement plans are far afield from each other.

- **Taxes.** Many retirees find their combined tax burden is less than it was during their working years, but this is not always the case. It is important to plan for this.

- **Automobile-related costs.** Retirees generally drive less than workers who commute to their jobs every day, thus spending less on maintenance, tolls, gasoline, etc.

- **Monthly contributions toward retirement savings accounts.** Not only can you stop making this contribution, you might even consider spending it!

- **Food.** This cost could go either way. If you think you will be eating out more, costs are likely to increase. If you plan on cooking more at home, costs can go down. I met a woman who used her time to plant a garden and saved thousands of dollars a year on food.

- **Clothing.** This is a cost that often goes down as dress shoes and other, more expensive attire are not needed as much.

- **Other Individual Needs.** Are your expenses on hobbies and other activities going to increase? Make sure to include them in your calculation.

SOURCES OF INCOME IN RETIREMENT

Now calculate the "paychecks" you'll receive. It's likely that if you have lived this long you're eligible for Social Security. You can go to your local Social Security Administration office or view your statement online at https://secure.ssa.gov/RIL/SiView.do.

Add the annual Social Security income amount, which will adjust for inflation, to any traditional pensions your employers have provided. Do you currently have a deferred annuity that will also provide income? Do you receive rental income? Add these to the final total.

THEN WHAT?

Once you analyze all this information, you can determine your estimated monthly income needs as well as how large of an emergency fund to establish. This fund should be held in a liquid and safe form and replenished by income as it becomes needed.

Consider reviewing your estimated needs at least annually, because circumstances can and do change in today's fast-moving world.

A KEY STEP

If you haven't already begun to work with an advisor who is a specialist in income-producing investments and instruments, this may be the time.

If you're considering doing it yourself, take some time to evaluate your expertise. Determine how much your time is worth. Will you be able to earn as much as the advisor specialist after their fee?

This is an important time to recognize your true strengths and weaknesses; there are no second chances in retirement.

If you have a relationship with an advisor, how well-suited are they for income-producing money management? Income investment is a specialty requiring research tools and trained and experienced analysts. Most financial planners don't have these skills. A good way to look at it is like this: If you have adult children, when they were born, they had a pediatrician. As your kids became adults, they probably changed doctors. If they didn't, I'm sure you would have strongly urged them to. Quite simply; their needs are different and they require someone more closely attuned to those needs. Getting on an adult scale relative to a baby scale indicates the need for different equipment as well. It's the same with income planning for retirement, or even during pre-retirement. I'm sure the pediatrician wasn't upset when they developed a more age-appropriate relationship, and your old financial planner should more than understand that your needs and goals have changed and it is time to adjust your strategy to support those goals. Another way to say this is: You wouldn't go to a podiatrist if you had a heart condition, would you? They are totally different specialties. Not all advisors are in the same bucket either. Make sure you have an income specialist for your retirement.

WHAT TO DO IF YOU'RE ALREADY RETIRED?

If you're already in retirement you have a little less control but still need to plan. If you're income is exceeding your expenses, try putting the excess away for a rainy day or other unforeseen circumstances.

I find many retirees have not made any plans to arrange their portfolios to reduce taxes, particularly when taking required minimum distributions (RMDs) out of retirement savings. Here are some of the things you should do to save money on RMD withdrawals.

Required Minimum Distributions

RMDs exist because the government also wants to make sure it can someday tax earnings that avoided taxes earlier in your life. If you have a 401(k), a Keogh, a SEP, or a traditional IRA, you are required to take minimum distributions (withdrawals) from your plan by April 1 of the year following the year in which you turn 70-and-a-half.

Even though the tax code allows you to wait until April 1 of the year following the year you turn 70-and-a-half, I advise clients to take their first mandatory withdrawal in the same year they reach that age. The reason is, waiting causes you to make two withdrawals in the first year. This has the effect of doubling the amount of taxable income you must declare. This is one potential tax savings just by following a little experienced advice. Not following it could potentially increasing your marginal tax bracket.

There are tables provided by the IRS and any good financial planning office should be able to calculate how much you are actually required to withdraw each year. What will be subject to taxation is based on tables that estimate your remaining lifetime.

Calculating Your Required Withdrawals

It can be very expensive if you don't maintain a disciplined process of taking minimum distributions from your qualified retirement plans. This is because the IRS really does want its money, so much so that if you miss taking the Required Minimum Distribution (RMD), the IRS will impose one of its highest penalties equal to 50 percent of the original RMD. This is another place where working with a professional can save you problems and real money.

How is it calculated? Based on your age, you simply divide your qualified plan balance as of the last day of the previous year by the factor from the IRS Publication 590 available here at: https://www.irs.gov/pub/irs-pdf/p590a.pdf.

Are Your Investment Allocations Right for Social Security?

It's advisable that you or your advisor determine your investments are as tax-efficient as possible for taking required or any other distributions in retirement.

As a general rule, take income out of taxable accounts first. This will leave more money earning deferred income, which will not only allow you to save more on taxes, but it can also grow and compound more as well.

Next, leave tax-exempt securities like municipal bonds as long as possible. If there is an option of selling a corporate bond or a municipal bond, under most situations the municipal bond should be held.

Roth IRAs should be the qualified money drawn from last. This is because you have already paid taxes on this money so what is left is earning or growing tax-free. Remember, managing your allocations and withdrawals is a matter of withdrawing tax-deferred assets only after taxable assets have been used and dipping into your tax-exempt funds only after the tax-deferred assets have been taken. However, a good retirement income plan should give you the confidence that you won't run out of money before you run out of life.

INDEX